Dee the
Business

Dee the Business

Peter K Fraser

BLACK & WHITE PUBLISHING

First published 2005
by Black & White Publishing Ltd
99 Giles Street, Edinburgh, EH6 6BZ

ISBN 1 84502 053 7

Copyright © Peter K Fraser 2005

A CIP catalogue record for this book is available
from the British Library.

Printed and bound by Nørhaven Paperback A/S

CONTENTS

INTRODUCTION   1

MANAGEMENT SYSTEMS   3
HOW IT ALL STARTED   3
BUSINESS CONCEPTS AND STANDARDS   14
A NORTH EAST VIEW OF THE IMPACT OF
   EXTERNAL STANDARDS   16

TERMINOLOGY AND CONTEXT   19
FINANCE   19
TRAVEL AND ACCOMMODATION   21
LEGAL   23
FARMING AND HORTICULTURE   25
OIL AND GAS   27
FASHION AND ENTERTAINMENT   28
NATIONAL HEALTH SERVICE   31
TELEVISION NEWS REPORTING   32
LOCAL TRANSPORT ISSUES   35

ADVICE AND 'BEST PRACTICE'   40
EDDIE DEMIN'S FOWERTEEN PYNTS   40
DEMING'S 'SYSTEM OF PROFOUND KNOWLEDGE'   44
HOW SOME DEFINITIONS DON'T HELP   47
WHAT IS A PROCESS?   50
WHAT WAS WRONG WITH THE OLD WAYS   53
HOW TO DESIGN A MANAGEMENT SYSTEM   57
MANAGEMENT LESSONS   61
LEADERSHIP TIPS   65
LEARNING LESSONS   68
HUMAN ERROR   70
PROBLEMS CAUSED BY POOR PROCEDURES   77
EDDIE'S SAX THINKIN BUNNETS   80

CONTENTS

5S	83
NEGATIVE ATTITUDES	85
POSITIVE ATTITUDES (PERSONAL MASTERY)	90
COMPUTERS AND TECHNOLOGY	96
MICROSOFT ERROR MESSAGES AND HAIKU POETRY	96
MICROSOFT ERROR MESSAGES	101
INFORMATION TECHNOLOGY AND BUSINESS SYSTEM TERMINOLOGY	104
TEXT MESSAGING IN THE NORTH-EAST	108
EMAIL ETIQUETTE	109
EMOTICONS	111
AND FINALLY . . .	114

Acknowledgements

With thanks to

My wife Mousie (née van de Scheur) –
for word-processing services beyond her
comprehension

Gordon Casely, journalist, of Herald Strategy Ltd –
for proof-reading and many constructive suggestions

and to
the loon fae Maud, Jack Webster –
for acknowledging the efforts of a grandson of a
Cyaaker (a resident of New Pitsligo)

To my father Sandy Fraser

FOREWORD

This is a fun book. Its target, often enough, is the world of business and management and not least that breed of so-called IT specialists who delight in having found a jargon to call their own. Sometimes they even want to keep it to themselves – preserving the mystique, as it were.

Of course some of that new-found language makes sense. Some more of it is simply gobbledygook. As Peter Fraser says, these people take themselves too seriously. So we are long overdue a bit of levity. And he provides it with the device of our own Doric dialect. That should throw them into some well-deserved confusion since our North-east tongue has its own complication of being a phonetic dialect. That means you spell it according to how to hear it, which is a recipe for variation if ever there was one. Whether you are stone-deaf, tone-deaf or just have some wax in your lugs, you are liable to come up with something different.

Those great Aberdeenshire poets Charles Murray and J. C. Milne – not to mention William Alexander and his *Johnny Gibb o' Gushetneuk* – heard it differently from, say, Robbie Shepherd in the modern world.

Sadly, we have lost our familiarity with the written Doric – and scarcely even speak it in a natural and everyday way any more. But let's not get too serious. Peter Fraser reminds us that the short, pithy Buchan phrase is often expressive in a way that English finds hard to match. Then there are times when the opposite applies and you can elongate a local phrase to farcical effect.

So you find here that the Doric definition of 'the bottom line' can emerge as 'fan yer knicker elastick's ower ticht'.

The author's father, the legendary Sandy Fraser, tried to teach me maths at Robert Gordon's College sixty years ago –

an' it wisna his wyte that he failed. A generation later, his son has a much better chance of raising a smile in this bewildering age when we need to lift our heads, take a good look around and discover that there's more to life than surfing, scrolling and texting.

Jack Webster

INTRODUCTION

Doric, the north-east tongue, makes it easy to express much in a few well-chosen words – *an tae mak a feel o hifalutin folk fa think they're Airchie jist cos they use funcy wirds fan they spik.* (and to make a fool of pompous people who think they are wonderful just because they use fancy words when they speak)

In 2004, I, as director of Aberdeen-based MandOS (Management & Operational Systems Ltd), published a Doric translation of the terminology used in the company's 'Promanade' management systems software when we introduced an enhancement for Chubb Insurance of London to allow users to customise the language used in the software. I was pleasantly surprised by the reaction from folk (not all from the north-east of Scotland) who found it both amusing and relevant. Appearances on BBC Radio and TV followed, the MandOS website had thousands of hits and I received e-mails from north-east folk around the world.

There is an unfortunate propensity for business people and academics to take themselves far too seriously and to create a language of their own which others can find daunting and unintelligible. This can be made worse when external standards and 'best practice' are presented in such a way as to confuse rather than to inform.

There is a place for an 'alternative view' of common business and IT terminology and jargon – and the fact that Doric lends itself to conveying much meaning in a few words makes it an ideal medium. The north-east attitude to grandiose opinions and inflated egos is also capable of accepting input from other languages. The late Lachie Simpson of the Granite City and Gordonian rugby clubs introduced the following (admittedly grammatically incorrect) phrase as a put-down. It soon became a catchphrase and T-shirt emblem as well:

Tomber le garcon!
Fa's the boy?
Who does he think he is?

Humour is too often missing from business and management discussions but put the two together and some powerful messages can be delivered. I leave it to you to decide which parts of the book are sensible, which get a useful message across and which bits are plain silly – bear in mind that even my friends don't take what I say too seriously!

Spelling in Doric can be difficult – different folk pronounce the same word in different ways in different parts of the northeast so there is no absolute 'correct' spelling in many cases. It sometimes works best if you don't try to analyse the spelling and just have a go at saying the words out loud.

An explanation of the Doric terms is provided for those readers unfamiliar with the language. So, if you want to know more, *it's time ti git yokit* (it's time to get started) – as in 'put the yoke on the horses and start ploughing'). *An, if ye're nae richt sure o fit it aa means, ye kin aye speir at onybody wi eneuch gumption ti ken – bit dinna ask ony feel gype (there's a fair few gyaan aboot).* And, if you are not completely sure of what it all means, you can always ask anyone with enough common sense to know – but don't ask any daft fool (there are more than a few around).

MANAGEMENT SYSTEMS

HOW IT ALL STARTED

The original translation into Doric of the field names and system messages in our Promanade software was prompted by the fact that many managers struggle to understand and apply the fundamentals of business process management to their own organisations. The terminology associated with the subject often makes simple concepts seem complex. But it is all basically to do with everyday work and personal interactions.

GENERAL

The wye ti dee things
The way to do things
▲ Process Flowcharts

The wye ti dee aathin
The way to do everything
▲ The entire system (explanatory text for link to the list of all processes)

Fit it's aa aboot
What it is all about
▲ 'Information' link on home page of published system

It's nae a list o baps, rowies, softies an nudgers
It's not a list of floury rolls, the famous Aberdeen butteries, soft buns and great loaves

ROLE REGISTER (List of Job Functions)

Bourachies o fowk
Groups of people
▲ Departments

Fit fowks' jobbies are caad
What people's jobs are called
▲ Roles (i.e. Job Titles)

Note: it is often convenient to include generic roles in the register, such as Nominated Person and Responsible Engineer. *Some fowk micht fin it handy ti hae NaeMe in the list an aa –* for the situation when something has gone wrong and the question is raised 'Who was responsible for this?' The answer is inevitably *'It wis NaeMe'.* NaeMe was, it is understood, heavily involved in the planning, design and construction management of the Scottish Parliament building.

Other possible role names include:

Deal chiel
Deal man
▲ Mergers and Acquisitions Specialist

(Aiberdeen) Angus
Mr Black
▲ Chief Operating Officer (COO)

Caff (chaff) chiel
Straw man

The late Mr Alexander (Eck) Utive
Executive

A director fa dis mair nor his fair share o gyaan aboot an shakkin
A company director who does more than his fair share of moving and shaking
▲ Keyboard Operator

A mannie fa pints cars
Carpenter

Hilly billie
Member of Aberdeen Mountain Rescue Team

Lily hilly billie
Member of Aberdeen Mountain Rescue Team who likes flower arranging

Tannie mannie
Tommy Sheridan (or, in a wider UK context, Robert Kilroy-Silk or Peter Hain) – or in Aberdeen fit ba terms, Jimmy Calderwood? ('fit ba heid bummer'?)

Tackitie teacake
Stud muffin

A stud wi nae finesse
Abrasive grinder

Laddie-da
Juvenile male parent

Wine quine
Female frequenter of No 10 Queens Terrace

Chuddy cuddy (nae eyven coos' moos are open fan they're chaain)
A chewing gum 'donkey' (not even cows' mouths are open when they are chewing)
▲ (Open-mouthed) gum chewer

Fanny mannie
A transsexual

Jeep neep
A 4x4 driver who stops on the double yellow lines to drop precious children off at the school gate

Moosie pussy
Mouser (cat employed to catch mice in a factory etc.)

Lug dug
Basset hound

RESOURCE REGISTER

A hanfu o handy things ti hae handy
A collection of useful things to have available
▲ Resource Group

Foo mony or foo muckle
How many or how much
▲ Value

Foo mony or foo muckle fit
How many or how much of what
▲ Unit of Measure

DOCUMENT REGISTER (List of Documents, Records and other Sources of Information)

Bumf
Paper or information
▲ Documents

Faur ti luik fir mair bumf
Where to look for more paper or information
▲ Document Register

Bourachies o bumf
Collections of paper. (Note: the term 'bourachie' tends to be used mostly for a gathering of people but I like the alliteration)
▲ Document Groups

Haud on til't fir . . .
Hold on to it for . . .
▲ Retention Period (for a Document or Record)

PROCESSES

Fit it's caad
What it is called
▲ Process Reference

Fit it's ti dee wi
What it is concerned with
▲ Process Title

Heid mannie
Head man (person who is accountable – or whose head is on the block if it goes wrong)
▲ Owner (of a Process or a Document)

Fa says 'aye'
Who say 'yes'
▲ Approver (of a Process)

Fit een
Which one
▲ Revision (Number of a Process)

Fan chyngit
When changed
▲ (Date a Process was last) revised

Faur ess een cam fae
Where this one came from
▲ Parent Process (for a Hyperlinked Sub-Process)

Nae quite feenisht
Not quite finished
▲ Draft (Version of a Process)

The wye ti dee things aat's richt up ti date
The way to do things that is right up to date
▲ Active (i.e. authorised) Version of Flowchart

Nae the wye ti dee things noo
Not the way to do things now
▲ Inactive (i.e. superseded) Version of Flowchart

TASKS (within a Process)

Jobbies or fit's deen
Pieces of work or what is done
▲ Tasks

Fit ti dee
What to do
▲ Task Title (preferably in verb-noun format)

The wye ti dee't
The way to do it
▲ Task Description

Fit neist? (Note: the best way to define a process is to define how things usually work – don't get hung up on all the 'what-ifs' which happen once in a blue moon)
What next?
▲ Sequence Number (of a Task within a Process)

Fit wye ye'd ging the ither wye
The reason you would go the other way
▲ Alternative Task Reason (for following a branch out of the normal Process Flow)

Fa dees't
Who does it
▲ Person Responsible (for a Task)

Telt
Told
▲ Informed

Speired at
Asked
▲ Consulted

Gies a haun til . . .
Gives a hand to . . .
▲ Assists

Fa's heid's on the block gin aathin gings erse ower tit
Whose head is on the block if everything goes awry
▲ The person accountable (for a Task or a Process)

Mak up
Make up
▲ Create (a Document or Record)

Gie a redd up til
Tidy up
▲ Update

Hae a lookie at
Have a look at
▲ Refer to

Pit awa
Put away
▲ File or Archive

GUIDANCE IN THE PUBLISHED
(ELECTRONIC) SYSTEM

'Gie a dunt ti the left lug o the moosie ower the heid o a bourachie o cairts ti the left ti hae a look at a list o the cairts in ahint it'

Press the left ear of the mouse over a process group to the left to look at a list of the maps (cards) behind it

▲ 'Left click on a Process Group at the left to display the List of Processes for that Process Group'

'There's nae a cairt gyaan aboot fir ess een'

There is not a map in circulation for this one

▲ 'A Flowchart is not currently available for this Process'

'It's bein chyngit – gie a dunt ti the left lug o the moosie here ti hae a keek at fit's goin oan wi it the noo'

It is being changed – press the left ear of the mouse here to have a quick look at what is happening to it at present

▲ 'It is currently under review – left click here to view a Draft Version of the Process Flowchart'

'Ess cairt's bein chyngit, bit ye canna hae a keek at it richt noo'

This map is being changed, but you can't view it at present

▲ 'This Process is currently under review, but a draft Flowchart is not currently available'

'Gie a dunt ti the left lug o the moosie here ti see the richt story'
Press the left ear of the mouse here to see the correct version
▲ 'Left click here to view the Issued Version of the Process Flowchart'

LINKS IN PUBLISHED PROCESSES

Anither cairt
Another map
▲ Sub-Process Hyperlink

Loup ti ess ither cairt
Jump to this other map
▲ Go to this Sub-Process (from a Hyperlink in the Process Map)

Hae a keek
Have a look
▲ Open this Document (from a Hyperlink in the Process Map)

Hae a keek at some mair bumf aboot the bumf
Have a look at some more information about the document
▲ Display Information about this Document (such as Retention Period, Owner, Where Used) from the Document Register

LINKS IN PUBLISHED DOCUMENT REGISTER

Gie a dunt ti the left lug o the moosie ower the heid o a bourachie o bumf ti hae a keek at aa the bumf in ahint it

Press the left ear of the mouse over a document group to the left to look at all the documents behind it

▲ Left click on a Document Group at the left to display the List of Documents for that Document Group

Mair o a story

More of a story

▲ Comments (free-format text to describe an entry in the Document Register)

REPORTS

Faur, fan an fit

Where, when and what (to do)

▲ Reference, Sequence Number and Process Title (in the heading of a Report listing Tasks within Processes)

Sneddit

Cut off

▲ Truncated (Task Description shown in a Summary Report)

Fit they dee

What they do

▲ Involvement (of a Specified Role)

Fit's deen neist

What is done next

▲ Task Sequence

Aa the keepit eens

All the owned ones

▲ Owned Processes (for a Specified Job Title)

Aa the 'aye' eens
All the approved ones
▲ Approved Processes (for a Specified Job Title)

Faur (an fit wye) the bumf's used
Where (and how) the document is used
▲ Document Usage Report

Mak't up bi . . .
Made up by . . .
▲ Created by . . .

Redd up bi . . .
Tidied up by . . .
▲ Updated by . . .

Lookit at bi . . .
Looked at by . . .
▲ Referred to by . . .

Pit awa bi . . .
Put away by . . .
▲ Filed by . . .

Fit ti dee – an fit wye an aa
What to do – and how, too
▲ Task Title/Description

Ticketyboo tick list
Checklist to provide evidence that everything has been completed (perfectly)
▲ Completion Checklist (for a Project)

Jobbie
A job (Note: the diminutive '-ie' ending is often to be found in the Doric – see also 'bitties' below)
▲ Project

Th'een fa shid dee't shid sign it aff fan it's deen
The one who should do it should sign it off when it is done
▲ The Responsible Person should sign off the appropriate Task(s) as they are completed

Fan it maun be deen afore
When it must be done before
▲ Due Date

Fan it wis deen
When it was done
▲ Date Completed

SYSTEM MESSAGES

The hale jing-bang pit thegither bi Promanade
The whole affair put together by Promanade
▲ Web Site generated by Promanade (footer on home page)

Aa the funcy bitties copyricht o MandOS
All the intricate details copyright MandOS
▲ Style, Design, Layout and Symbols copyright MandOS (footer on home page)

BUSINESS CONCEPTS AND STANDARDS

Fit wye a thingie's fit fir an fit it's supposed ti fit
The way in which something is suitable for it's intended purpose
▲ Quality

Fit ye're fit fir
What you are capable of
▲ Competency

***Fit gings oot the windae if ye mischieve yersel – or
ither fowk***
What is lost or compromised if you cause damage or
injury to yourself – or other people
▲ Health and Safety
(Note: in 'mischieve', the emphasis is on the last
syllable)

Onythin aat kin mak an erse o fit ye're tryin ti dee
Anything which can make a real mess of what you are
trying to do
▲ Business Risk

Handy things ti hae handy
Convenient or useful things to have at hand
▲ Resources

***Onythin aat kin affeckt fit wye ye git ti faur ye're
gyaan or fit wye ye ging***
Anything that can affect which way you get to where
you are going or the way you get there
▲ Influence

***The mair gypit prices siccan £9.99 ye git in the shoppies,
the mair chynge aabody his ti stotter aboot wi. Aa yon
1p pieces in yer pooch wid fair deeve onybody***
***An it's jist the same in business – ither folk dee things
aat mak ye rehash fit wye ye cairry oan yirsel***
The more prices such as £9.99 you get in shops, the
more change everyone has to stumble around with. All
those 1p pieces in your pocket are bound to bother
anyone

And it is just the same in business – other people do
things which make you revise and redesign the way you
operate
▲ Managing Change

*Fit ye think aat ither fowk dee – or, if ye're flannelin,
fit ye say ye dee yersel*
What you think that other people do – or, if you are
unrestrained in claims about your own performance,
what you say you do yourself
▲ Best Practice

*Aboot as muckle eese as an erse set in concrete – ye
kin mebbe park yer bike atween the chicks bit ye're
awa doon at the wee jobbie livel (in mair wyes an
een?) an maist fowk dinna twig aat fit they're deein is
pairt o a muckler picter*
About as much use as a rear-end set in concrete – you
can perhaps park your bicycle between the cheeks but
you are away down at the small task level (in more
ways than one?) and most people don't realise that
what they are doing is part of a bigger picture
▲ Bottom-Up Process Mapping

A NORTH-EAST VIEW OF THE IMPACT OF EXTERNAL STANDARDS

Japanese-style Haiku poetry has strict construction rules. Each
poem has only seventeen syllables and three lines – five syllables in the first line, seven in the second, five in the third.
Haikus are used to communicate a timeless message often
achieving a wistful, yearning and powerful insight through
extreme brevity – the essence of Zen.

Yir fowk maitter maist?
They maun aa be affa chufft!
Sae fit wye sack em?
Your staff matter most?
They must all be very pleased!
So why the layoffs?
▲ IIP (Investors in People)

Ye 'dee' quality?
Customers fair teen wi ye?
Dinna mak me lauch.
You 'do' quality?
Customers are pleased with you?
Please don't make me laugh.
▲ ISO9001 (Quality Management)

Chummin wi the Greens?
Nae hairm ti nithin noo. Sae
Fit wye the rin-affs?
In the green lobby?
Damage to nothing now. So
Why the waste and spills?
▲ ISO14001 (Environmental Management)

Myn oot fir us aa –
Or sae aa yer bumf aye says.
Fa's mischieved the day?
Mind out for us all –
Or so your paperwork says.
Who is injured today?
▲ ISO18001 (Occupational Health and Safety
   Management)

Nae bairns up the lum?
Aabody chufft wi their pye?
Bit foo div ye buy?
No young chimney sweeps?
Everyone pleased with their pay?
But how do you buy?
▲ SA8000 (Social Accountability)

Chunce o a chuncer?
Siller at risk? Sae ye spen
Mair noo – aye a chunce!
Chance of a 'chancer'?
Money at risk? So you spend
More now – chance remains!
▲ Sarbanes-Oxley Act (SOX)

Troo naebody noo.
Spell oot fit wye ye dee things
An hank it aa doon.
Believe no one now.
Spell out how you operate
And tie it all down.
▲ Sarbanes-Oxley Act (SOX)

TERMINOLOGY AND CONTEXT

A recurring problem with narrative descriptions of work and business operations is that the same word or phrase has different meanings for different people. Some examples are given in the following pages.

FINANCE

Birlin the pedals lik b*gg*ry
Turning the pedals very quickly
▲ Operating Cycle

A said, 'A'm deen't.'
I said, 'I'm doing it.'
▲ Operating Statement

Neen o thae new-fangelt text messages fir me
None of those modern text messages for me
▲ Invoice

A said, 'Neen o thae new-fangelt text messages fir me.'
I said, 'None of those modern text messages for me.'
▲ Statement

'Hing the criminal' 6 / 'He widna hurt a flech' 6
'Hang the criminal' 6 / 'He wouldn't hurt a flea' 6
▲ Trial balance

Fan ye fairly dinna wint ti be the spikker fa's oan richt aifter they've hid their denner
When you certainly don't want to be the speaker who is on right after lunchtime
▲ Accounting convention

An ill lick
A bad speed
▲ Accrual rate

Jeemy (Twa Nithins Sivvin) – gie't a shak an pit yer spurtle awa fir ony sake
James (007) – shaken not stirred
▲ Bond

CHIELS
CHAPS beef cattle

Aiberdeen Angus
Beef cattle
▲ Convertible stock

Fit the Cod Crusaders hiv – bit mebbe the Scottish Executive hisna
What the campaigners for the Scots fishing industry have – but perhaps not the Scottish Executive
▲ Net interest

PREEN
PIN
▲ Personal Identification Number

Fit free-range hens dee
What free-range hens do
▲ Outlay

Spik aboot the draaer
Talk about the drawer
▲ Refer to drawer

Plowt an Judy?
Punch and Judy?
▲ Show of hands

Buy a buttery
Purchase an Aberdeen roll
▲ Payroll

Fit hauds up a fince
What holds up a fence
▲ Post

A fit aat gits pyed
A foot which has abandoned amateur status
▲ Profit

Fit happens ti the beasts gin it's rainin an they canna git in aboot ti the cattle-coort
What happens to the cattle if it is raining and they can't get access to the cowshed
▲ Shrinkage

A'm nae askin, A'm telling ye – pit yer haun in yer pooch richt noo
I'm not asking, I'm telling you – come up with the cash right now
▲ Purchase order

TRAVEL AND ACCOMMODATION

Jist fit ye wint ti howk a hole fir yersel
Just what you want (a spade) to dig a hole for yourself
▲ Signal Passed at Danger (SPAD)

A funcy piece an a drink ti combine oan the combine
A fine cake and a drink to combine on the harvester
▲ Fly-drive package

Fit they tak aff ye afore ye tak aff
What they take off you before you take off
▲ Airport tax

Fit taks ye aff fan ye land
What takes you off when you land
▲ Airport taxi

A tea jenny
A devotee of the fly cup
▲ Frequent flier

A quine fa winna lee ye alane – a bittie lik a bad case o plooks
A girl who won't leave you alone – rather like a bad case of spots
▲ Near miss

Password fir a spaver
Password for a man's trouser fly
▲ Zip code

A pyoke o nieves, fingers (rhymes with 'singers') an thooms
A parcel of fists, fingers and thumbs
▲ Hand luggage

Huddin yer thoom an yer crannie up i the air aside yer lug
Holding your thumb and your little finger up beside your ear
▲ Call sign

'Scotlan the Fit' hiv jist caad aff
The (well-known north-east comedy group) 'Scotland the What' has just called off
▲ No-show

Fit dee ye git if ye cross a road wi a barra? Knockit doon, if ye dinna hash on
What do you get if you cross a road with a wheelbarrow? Knocked down, if you don't hurry

Hurlie Davidson
An upmarket wheelbarrow
▲ Hurley Davidson

Is yon mannie fit ti flee?
Fit ti fit?
Flee.
Foo fit's he?
He's fou.
Foo fou?
He's fleein.
Then he's nae fleein the day.

Is that gentleman in a suitable condition to be admitted to the aeroplane?
Fit to do what?
Fly.
How fit is he?
He's inebriated.
How inebriated?
Extremely inebriated.
Then he's not getting on this flight today.

LEGAL

A'd hae bade in ma bed if A'd kent fit wis in store fir the rest o the day
I would have stayed in my bed if I had known what was in store for the rest of the day
▲ Affidavit

Ae draawer
One drawer
▲ A brief

Fit ye jist hae ti dee fin onybody is ower bumptious
What you just *have* to do when anyone is very full of themselves
▲ Compulsory winding up

Nae an NHS duntist – it's lik draain teeth ti git onybody ti draa teeth in the north-east nooadays
Not an NHS dentist (it's like drawing teeth to get anybody to draw teeth in the north-east these days)
▲ Drawer

Nae yon craa ower there
Not that crow over there
▲ Escrow

The loon's awa ti the Far East
The boy is away to the Far East
▲ Euthanasia

Fit jist a pucklie fowk hae ti dee
What only a small number of people must do
▲ Feu duty

Chums oan a nicht oot fa dinna hae much gyaan fir them
Friends on a night out who don't have much going for them
▲ Limited company

Stag nicht cairry-oans
Stag night frivolity
▲ Manslaughter

Aitkens the Baker
The king of Aberdeen bakers
▲ Master of the Rolls

Fit?
What?
▲ Pardon

Fit a mannie pynts at the porcelain
What a gentleman points at a toilet bowl
▲ Per se

Jist the same as ilka Saiterday nicht – A wis ragin aat ma denner wisna ready fan a got hame fae the pub
Just the same as every Saturday night – I was very annoyed that my dinner was not ready when I got home from the pub
▲ Plaintiff

Nae movin, onywye
Not moving, anyway
▲ Deed

If ye say ye're deid, ye're deid, as faur as A'm concerned
If you say you are dead, you are dead, as far as I am concerned
▲ Deed of Trust

FARMING AND HORTICULTURE

Crap
Crop – the yield from a growing or cultivation process

The crap's fair spylt wi aa ess rain
The crop is completely spoiled with all this rain

The word can also be applied to any business process and its outcome – especially by the less enlightened manager or the less committed worker.

> ***Fit neep's responsible fir aa ess crap?***
> Which turnip is responsible for this collective outcome?
> (Note: there is often a direct correlation between the
> skills, resources, planning and preparation put into a
> process and the quality of the output from it.)

In the European context, the concept can be further extended to the Common Agricultural Policy (CAP).

> ***CRAPs wi nae Rs (sae faur did it cam fae?)***

(HEAVY) PLANT CROSSING

> ***Fit div ye get gin ye cross an ingin wi a neep? A daft
> gowk fa'd gaar ye greet.***
> What do you get if you cross an onion with a turnip? A
> silly fool who would make you cry.

> ***Fit div ye get gin ye cross a rose wi a beetreet? A wee
> reid prick.***
> What do you get if you cross a rose with a beetroot? A
> small red prick.

> ***Fit div ye get gin ye cross a cubbage wi a rasp? An affa
> noisy guff in yer lug.***
> What do you get if you cross a cabbage with a
> raspberry? A very noisy smell in your ear.

> ***Fit div ye get gin ye cross a beet wi a French cubbage?
> Funcy fitweer – boot/choux.***
> What do you get if you cross a beet with a French
> cabbage? Fancy footwear – boot/shoe.

OIL AND GAS

Kim awa ben, Camilla, quine
Come away in, Camilla, my girl
▲ Advance Royalty

Pump
Break wind
▲ Blowout

A'm feart o giein maasel fern-ticklt draaers – A hid a curry last nicht
I am afraid of giving myself freckled underpants – I had a curry last night
▲ Blowout preventer

Fit A git gin A'm feart o giein maasel fern-ticklt draaers
What I get if I am afraid of giving myself freckled underpants
▲ Bottom-Hole Pressure

A bit o tow ti haud yer dreels in a stracht line
A piece of string to keep your (garden) drills in a straight line
▲ Drill string

Ile Park
oil Field
▲ oil Field

Rod
Angler's equipment
▲ Fishing tool

Roddie
Wee Roderick
▲ Fishing-tool operator

A wye ti mak a hash o things thegither
A way to make a (drug-induced?) mess of things together
▲ Joint Venture

Tattie
Potato
▲ Spud

We'll mak oan aat we're ahint ye aa the wye – or ye mak a cuddy o somethin
We will indicate that we are behind you all the way – until you make a mess of something
▲ Empowerment

FASHION AND ENTERTAINMENT

Bosie cosy
Bosom warmer
▲ Boob tube

Breestie bowster
Breast bolster
▲ Padded bra

Fit a quine ends up wi if she disna hae a breestie bowster nor a bosie cosy
What a girl ends up with if she foregoes superstructure support
▲ Bouncers

Claas
Claws
▲ False nails

Gulls' skitters
Seagulls' droppings
▲ Hair highlights

Flooer o Thcotlan
Flower of Thcoland
▲ Thong

Faither's coo
Father's cow
▲ Pop socks

Pechin
Breathing heavily
▲ Short pants

A wee chick – or mebbe a short-ersed trappie
A small chicken – or perhaps a female conquest of less
than Amazonian proportions
▲ Pullet

Fit a foon ba heid's cover'd wi
What a base ball head is covered with
▲ Baseball cap on a skinhead

**Shell-suit breeks? A've seen her frae ahint an there's
nae wye aat she'll suit onythin ither nor a tint!**
Shell-suit bottoms? I have seen her rear view, and
there is no way that she'll suit anything other than
a tent!

**Ower pit-on pint aa ower – hiv ye seen yon quines fa
clart themsels wi eneuch cresote aat wid preserve wid
fir eers?**
Excessively applied paint all over – have you seen those
girls who apply enough fake tan to preserve wood for
years?
▲ (Over-applied) fake tan on a whole-body basis

*An it's nae affa bonny ti see a lassie's belly gyaan aa lon-
gitudinal ower the tap o her breeks. Fit wye div they nae
mak sarks lang eneuch sae aat quines kin tuck them in?*
And it's not very attractive to see a young girl's stomach
sagging over the top of her trousers. Why do they not
make shirts long enough so that they can be tucked in?

A lad fae Caithness wi an eye fir the quines
A young man from the far north of Scotland who takes
a keen interest in the opposite sex
▲ Tongue stud

Perhaps he uses the (less-than-subtle) approach to the fairer
sex exemplified by the following chat-up lines recounted to me
by my best man Doug Johnston from his former classmates –
perhaps the subsequent typhoid outbreak in Aberdeen was
God's retribution.

'Nivver myn the stars – drap yer draaers.'
'Nivver myn the moon – get em doon.'
'Damn the caul an frost – ma willie's lost.'

*An div ye nae think aat yon muckle roch-lookin
limousines ye see gyaan aboot mist be a franchise fae
Henry Thomson the floater fae Sauchen? Bi the luik o
the quines fa git coupit oot on tae the Boulie ti get
their picters teen, mebbe 'limo' is short fir 'limousin',
nae 'limousine'. (If ye hae a lookie at their shooders,
maist o them hiv been brandit.)*
And do you not think that those large vulgar 'stretch
limos' you see going about must be a franchise from
Henry Thomson, the livestock transportation specialists
in Aberdeenshire? By the look of the ladies who are
emptied out on to the Beach Boulevard to have their
photograph taken, perhaps 'limo' is an abbreviation for
'limousin' rather than 'limousine'. (If you look at their
shoulders, most of them have tattoos.)

NATIONAL HEALTH SERVICE

DEGREES OF ILLNESS IN GRAMPIAN

Nae affa weel
Not very well

Nae weel
Ill

Affa nae weel
Seriously ill

Weally weel
The state of extweemely good health enjoyed by those
who don't pronounce their Rs

MEDICINE

Fit's fit ti fit ti fit fit's tae?
What is suitable to attach to which foot's toe?
▲ Technical challenge for an orthotics specialist,
   chiropodist or elocutionist

Yer heid's leakin
Dampness is affecting your head
▲ Braindump

PHYSICAL FITNESS

Dee ess at least fower days a wik:
Do this at least four days a week:

*Afore ye git yokit, mak siccar aat ye hiv a bittie space
aroon ye.*
Before you start, make sure that you have enough space
around you.

Tak a 5lb tattie seck in ilka hun, pit baith airms oot stracht fae yer shooders and hud them up fir as lang as ye kin. A hale minutie wid dee an then hae a bit rest.
Take a 5lb potato sack in each hand, put both arms out straight from your shoulders and hold them up for as long as you can. A whole minute would do and then have a rest.

Ilka day, ye'll munnage a bittie langer. Aifter mebbe twa wikks, ging up ti 10lb tattie secks. Ca awa until ye kin dee't wi 50lb tattie secks an mebbe eyven git sae aat ye kin dee it wi 100lb tattie secks in ilka hun.
Each day, you will manage a little longer. After perhaps two weeks, go up to 10lb potato sacks. Keep going until you can do it with 50lb potato sacks and perhaps even get so that you can do it with 100lb potato sacks in each hand.

Fan ye're comfy wi aat, pit ae tattie in ilka seck – bit ca affa canny gin ye rax yersel.
When you are comfortable with that, put one potato in each sack – but very careful in case you strain yourself.

TELEVISION NEWS REPORTING

We're nae lang yokit, an A've nae tell't ye muckle yit bit we think aat ye canna concentrate fir mair nor twa-three minuties at a time an, maist important fir us, it means we dinna hae ti scutter aboot an fin mair claik ti fill the programme wi gin we say the same thing ower an ower agin.
We have hardly started and I haven't told you much yet but we think that you can't concentrate for more than two or three minutes at a time and, most importantly

for us, it means that we don't have to waste time to find more stories with which to fill the programme if we say the same thing over and over again.

There's jist ae wye ti mak life eyven easier fir us – git aa ye gypes ti send's texts an emails, an we jist sit oan wir doups an read them aa oot again. We kin mak hale programmes ess wye. Sillar fir aul tow!

There is just one way to make life even easier for us – get all you unthinking simpletons to send us texts and emails and we just sit on our backsides and read them out again. We can make whole programmes this way. Money for old rope!

▲ Still to come in the rest of the programme

A ken nithin'll hae chyngit – it nivver dis – bit A'll jist say it aa ower agin fir the sake o't.

I know nothing will have changed – it never does – but I'll say it all over again for the sake of it.

▲ I'll be back a little later with an update on the main news stories

A'm a parrot fa disna think aboot fit A'm sayin. There's nae wye we cwid hae aa yon billies spikkin at ae time – it's BBC Scotland or nithin fir you fowk. Div ye expeck me ti think an spik at ae time?

I am a parrot who does not think about what I am saying. There is no way we could have all those people speaking at one time – it's BBC Scotland or nothing for you people. Do you expect me to think and speak at the same time?

▲ Now it's time to join our news teams around the country – bye for now.

A ken aat you fowk pey the licence fee bit A'm gyaan ti turn ma back oan ye fir a filie an hae a blether wi a

*mannie oan a screen ahint me. Ma chum Jay Spurgie'll
turn her back an aa, sae aat it's as if aa you fowk dinna
maitter ava.*

I know that you people pay the licence fee, but I am
going to turn my back on you for a while and speak to
a man on a screen behind me. My colleague Ms Bird
will turn her back as well so that it's as if you people
don't matter at all.

▲ Let's speak to our correspondent in . . .

*Ye can aye hae a leuk at aa the oangyaans in ahint –
there's aye a pucklie screens flicherin an a mannie or
twa gyaan awa fir a fly an ye kin coont up foo mony
skyrie colours we've pit intil the hale picter. It fair taks
yer min awa fae fit we're spikkin aboot.*

You can always have a look at all the goings-on behind
– there are always a few screens flickering and one or
two people going away for a cup of tea and you can
count up how many gaudy colours we have put into
the whole picture. It certainly takes your mind off what
we are speaking about.

DODDIE TWA SHEEP

It has been confirmed that the following message was never
sent by George W Bush to John Porter when he was elected
leader of the local Tory group on Aberdeen City Council.

*A'm fair forfochenated at the wye aa ye
Aiberdeenonians an Buchaneers spik. If A used wirdin-
ology lik aat in the Fite Hoosie, mah ain kintraladdies
and lassiefowks in the USoA wid hae nae chunce o
kennin fit A'm spikkinatin aboot.*

I am quite perplexed at the way you residents of
Aberdeen and Buchan speak. If I used terminology like

that in the White House, my own countrymen and – women would have no chance of understanding what I am speaking about.

A ken aat Aiberdeen is kent the world ower as the oil capitalisation o Europe and ye've hid hale bourirachies o Yunkies in toon fir the lest 30 years noo. Myn ye, yon Saddam Hussie wis the maist bour o aa the Irachies in ma myn. Ye ken, ae lad did say eence aat he thocht A wis in twa minds – losh, A'm nae richt sure aat A hae eyven een aat works richt!

I know that Aberdeen is known the world over as the oil capital of Europe and you have had large numbers of Americans in town for the last 30 years now. Mind you, that Saddam Hussein was the worst of the Iraqis in my mind. You know, one person did say once that he thought that I was in two minds – goodness, I am not totally convinced that I have even one in full working order!

Onywye, greetins til ye aa in Aiberdeen stracht frae the presidential mou – aat should be eneuch ti gaar a grown mannie greet!

Anyway, best wishes to you all in Aberdeen straight from the Presidential mouth – that should be enough to make any grown man reach for a handkerchief!

LOCAL TRANSPORT ISSUES

ABERDEEN'S INTEGRATED TRANSPORT POLICY

Jist hae a look at the Lang Stracht in Aiberdeen – there's a bittie o aathin aa in ae road. There's a wee bittie fir cyclists, pucklies o bus lanes aawye (an neen

mair than a fyowe yairds lang), files there's ae lane fir cars an larries an files there's twa an, ti add ti the mixter-maxter, there's traffic lichts aa ower the place.
Just have a look at the Lang Stracht in Aberdeen – there is a bit of everything all in one road. There is a short stretch for cyclists, small portions of bus lanes everywhere (and none of them more than a few yards long). Sometimes there is a lane for cars and lorries and sometimes there are two and, to add to the mixture, there are traffic lights all over the place.

As fir kennin fit lane ti ging intil, mak siccar aat ye tichen yer yoke – there's twa lanes fir a stairt bit syne een turns intil a bus lane, sae ye hae ti haud ti yer richt. Syne, the een yer in noo is jist fir turnin richt. Sae the richt lane is nae the richt lane if ye're gyaan richt on. Bit if ye need ti ging richt ye're aa richt.
As far as knowing which lane to go in, make sure that you put on your seatbelt – there are two lanes for a start but then one of them turns into a bus lane so you have to keep to your right. Later, the one you are in now is just for turning right. So the correct lane is not the right lane if you are going straight on. But if you need to go right you are all right.

Sae myn an caa the wheel ower ti the left a bittie aifter yer past the bus lane – bit dinna dee't ower soon sae aat the cooncil kin tak a photie o yer nummerplate an tak some sillar aff ye (een gin there's nae a bussie in sicht). An keep yir een peelt fir ony loons peddlin awa wi their breeks tuckit intil their socks an a dirler oan their heids.
So remember to pull the wheel over to the left a bit after you are passed the bus lane – but don't do it too soon so that the council can take a photograph of your

number plate and fine you (even if there is not a bus in sight). And keep your eyes peeled for any young men peddling away with their trousers tucked into their socks and a (chamberpot) cycle helmet on their heads.

An gin ye kin spy a bus (aat'll fair gie ye a fleg!), hae a coont o the fowk sittin inaboot if it's een o yon bendy buses – there's a prize gin ye see mair nor sivvin.
And if you actually notice a bus (that will fairly give you a fright!), count the number of people sitting inside if it is one of those articulated buses – there is a prize if you see more than seven.

CYCLING

It's nae aat easy ti haud fowk aathigither peddlin awa on their bikes wi cars aat are parkit – hae a lookie on the North Deeside Road an ye'll see fit we mean. Een gin ye git a gweed rin at it oan yer bike wie nae cars in sicht, there's aye a puckle muckle holes aat wid rax yer knuckles an gaar yer wheels buckle.
It is not that easy to integrate cyclists with parked cars – if you have a look on the North Deeside Road and you will see what we mean. Even if you get a good run at it on your bike with no cars in sight, there are always a few big holes that would strain your knuckles and buckle your wheels.

Ye'd think aat Aiberdeenshire Cooncil wid hae decent roads fir cyclists, seein aat the Cooncil's heid bummer is a weel-kent peddler himsel. There's aat mony pot-holes aat ye'd need an affa strong erse ti ging far on their bit roadies. Sayin aat, myn, there's twa-three fowk fa follow him fa've said, 'Ere's an erse aheid.' Is aat fit wye he's caad the 'heid bummer'?

You would think that Aberdeenshire Council would have decent roads for cyclists, given that the Council's Chief Executive is himself a well-known cyclist. There are so many potholes that you would need a very substantial backside to go far on their roads. Saying that, mind you, there are a few people who follow him who have said, 'There's a backside ahead.' Is that why he is called the '—'?

PLANNING

In April 2005, Aberdeen City Council erected signs at the bottom end of Union Street saying, 'ACCESS RESTRICTED – FOOTWAY IMPROVEMENTS'.

Fit wye a 'fitwye' improvement? Fit's adee wi 'pavements'? Myn you, there maun be somethin wrang wi them – aat's fit wye ye canna access them.
Why a 'footway' improvement? What is wrong with 'pavements'? Mind you, there must be something wrong with them – that's why you can't access them.

Aabody kens aat the A96 (Aiberdeen ti Inverskeckaleekie) is an affa road – aat's fit wye fowk are sae keen oan getting a byepass biggit fir ilka village an toon on the wye. Sae fit wye are oor local cooncillers gyaan in the ither direction oan the A944? Jist ootbye at Elrick, oan fit his aye bin the main road til Alford an aa pynts west (Co-opie Doug's an aa), they biggit a muckle roonaboot aat an artic couldna ging roon – an aa the time they gie the thooms up ti mair and mair hooses aa roon aboot. Jyned up thinkin? Foo lang wil't be afore Elrick is needin a byepass an aa?
Everyone knows that the A96 (Aberdeen to Inverness) is a terrible road – that's why people are so keen on

getting a bypass built for every village and town on the way. So why are our local councillors going in the other direction on the A944? Just out near Elrick, on what has always been the main road to Alford and all points west (the Mossat shop included), they built a large roundabout which an articulated lorry could not go round – and all the time they give approval to more and more houses all around. Joined up thinking? How long will it be before Elrick is in need of a bypass as well?

ADVICE AND 'BEST PRACTICE'

Some of the 'expert' advice and opinion on offer to managers can mystify rather than assist understanding. We suspect that this happens sometimes because the author is trying to make his or her 'knowledge' sound grander and more impressive than it actually is. In such cases, 'simplicity lies beyond complexity' – true understanding is demonstrated by the ability to get the message across in a way which clarifies rather than confuses . . .

EDDIE DEMIN'S FOWERTEEN PYNTS

Dr W. Edwards Deming was an American statistician who contributed significantly to the post-war quality revolution in Japan in the 1950s and in the West in the 1980s and 1990s. His fourteen action points for management (from his book *Out of the Crisis*) are designed to achieve transformation from the present style of management to one of optimisation.

> *1 Caa awa thegither ti mak aathin better fir aabody.*
> Drive forward together to make things better for everyone.
> ▲ Create constancy of purpose toward improvement of product and service, with the aim to become competitive and to stay in business and to provide jobs.

2 Gie yer heid a richt gweed redd-up. There's a pucklie new-fangelt noshuns gyaan aboot. Aa they heid bummer chiels maun gie thirsels a richt gweed shak.

Give your head a good tidy-up. There are some new ideas going about. All the manager folk need to give themselves a good shake.

▲ Adopt the new philosophy. We are in a new economic age. Western management must awaken to the challenge, must learn their responsibilities and take on the leadership of change.

3 Dee awa wi pernickety fowk geein aathin the eence-ower. Dee it richt first time.

Do away with fastidious people giving everything the once-over.

▲ Cease dependence on inspection to achieve quality. Eliminate the need for inspection on a mass basis by building quality into the product in the first place.

4 Savin a pucklie bawbees iv noo disna aye win in the lang rin.

Saving a few ha'pennies now doesn't always give the best result in the long run.

▲ End practice of awarding business on the basis of price tag, instead minimise total cost. Move toward a single supplier for any one item, on a long-term relationship of loyalty and trust.

5 Dinna stan still – ye kin aye dee things better.

Don't stand still – you can always do things better.

▲ Improve constantly and forever the system of production and service, to improve quality and productivity and thus constantly reduce costs.

6 Gie fowk a haun ti learn the best wye ti dee their wirk.

Help people to learn the best way to do their work

▲ Most workers can't do their jobs because no one tells them how and they learn from watching others who may not be role models. Institute training on the job.

7 Get the heid bummers ti hae a think aboot faur they're gyaan, fit wye they're gyaan aboot it an fit wye they kin help folk ti dee it aa better.

Get managers to think about where they are going, how they are going about it and how they can help people to do it all better.

▲ Institute Leadership (see point TWELVE). The aim of leadership should be to help people and machines and gadgets to do a better job. Leadership of management is in need of overhaul, as well as leadership of production workers

8 Mak siccar aat fowk are nae feart ti dee things, say things or spier at ye sae aabody rugs thegither.

Make sure that people aren't afraid to do things, say things or ask you questions so that everyone pulls together.

▲ Drive out fear so that everyone may work effectively for the company.

9 Mak siccar aat fowk ging thegither fir the richt rizzons – sae aat they kin aa wirk thegither. Nae sacrit coos ahint dykes.

Make sure that people get together for the right reasons – so that they can all work together. No sacred cows behind walls.

▲ Break down barriers between departments. People in research, design, sales and production must work as

a team, to foresee problems of production and in use
that may be encountered with the product or
service.

**10 Fowk'll jist girn gin ye blether on aboot gypit goals
an dinna gie them fit they need ti dee fit needs ti be
deen.**
People will just complain if you spout about silly goals
and don't give them the resources they need to do what
is required of them.
▲ Eliminate slogans, exhortations and targets for work
force asking for zero defects and new levels of
productivity.

**11 Dee awa wi tairgets. The heid bummer should aye
be geein fowk a haun ti dee things better.**
Do away with targets. The boss should always be
helping people to do things better.
▲ Eliminate management by objective. Eliminate
management by numbers, numerical goals. Eliminate
work standards (quotas) on the factory floor.
Substitute leadership.

**12 Mak it easy fir fowk ti hae a gweed conceit o
themselves.**
Make it easy for people to have a good opinion of
themselves.
▲ Remove barriers that rob people of their right to
pride of workmanship. This means, inter alia,
abolition of the annual or merit rating and of
management by objective, management by numbers.
The responsibility of supervisors must change from
sheer numbers to quality.

13 Dinna haud back learnin. Get yer heid roon fit wye fit happens an fit ye dee fits wi fit's gyaan oan roon aboot.

Don't stop learning. Get your head round the way in which what happens and what you do fits with what is going on around you.

▲ Institute a vigorous program of education and self-improvement.

14 Mak siccar aat naebody hauds back fae gyaan forrit.

Make sure that nobody holds back from going forward.

▲ Put everyone to the task. Put everyone in the company to work to accomplish the transformation. Transformation is everybody's job.

DEMING'S 'SYSTEM OF PROFOUND KNOWLEDGE'
(with thanks to Gordon Hall of the
Deming Learning Network)

Dr W Edwards Deming describes the four inter-related aspects of knowledge necessary for transformation of the prevailing style of management in the West as:

● Appreciation of a system
● Knowledge about variation
● Theory of knowledge
● Psychology

You do not need to be eminent in any one part to understand it and apply it. The fourteen action points for management, as outlined in the previous section, follow naturally as the application of this knowledge. The various segments of this system of profound knowledge cannot be separated.

Seein the hale picter: ye need aa the bitties (fowk, stuff, ingines an wyes o deein) ti wirk thegither ti gie the tairgit a richt gweed skelp.

Seeing the whole picture: you need all the pieces (people, material, machinery and methodologies) to work together to give the target a good hit.

▲ Appreciation of a system: A system is a series of functions or activities within an organisation that works together for the aim of the organisation. It is a network of people, materials, methods, equipment, all working together so all benefit. When every part is working in support of every other part there is optimisation.

There's aye traivel in aathin: nithin's ivver 'jist so' – it's aye a pucklie mair nor a pucklie less. If aathin gings a bit shooglie, speir at yersel fit wye is't happinin. Is't the wye ye're deein things or his an inabootcomer pit his fit intilt? Gin it's the first een, dee it better! Gin it's t'ither, dinna ficher aboot wi the wye ye dee things – ye'll jist makt waur.

There is movement in everything: nothing is ever 'just so' – it is always a bit more or a bit less. If things become unsteady, ask yourself why it is happening. Is it the way you are doing things or has an outside influence disrupted things? If it is the first one, do it better! If it is the other, don't tamper – you'll just make it worse.

▲ Knowledge about variation: There will always be variation amongst people, output, service, products etc. All data collected contains variation. Systems can be stable and contain expected variation or can be unstable with unexpected variation. Management reaction to expected and unexpected variation should be very different. With expected variation, you should improve the process or system. With unexpected variation, you should seek to identify the cause of the instability. It is a common (and costly) mistake to fail to differentiate between these two types of variation.

Dinna jalouse: ye maun unnerstan fit shid be the wye o things, foonit oan fit ye ken o fit wis the wye o't afore. Don't guess: you must understand what should be the way of things, based on what you know of what has happened before.

▲ Theory of knowledge: Our actions and the methods we employ evolve out the basis of our thinking. Which, if we are seeking improvement, leads us to two options:
  ▲ we can stay with our existing thinking and improve methods and their application
  ▲ we can challenge the basis of our thinking, our theoretical assumptions.

The theory of knowledge teaches us to be aware of the basis of our thinking, acknowledging that it may be out of date. New theoretical assumptions may have been developed that have a far greater potential for engaging the commitment and creativity of staff. Furthermore, management is about prediction. 'If, from this theoretical assumption, I take that action, then I predict an outcome.' Theory of knowledge teaches us a learning discipline where we review outcomes relative to both method and theory applied. We build knowledge through systematic revision and extension of theory based on comparison of prediction with observation.

Fit wye fowk fit in wi ither fowk: – fit maks em dee fit they dee. Fit scunners em an fit maks them wint ti dee better.

How people fit in with other people: – what makes them do what they do. What frustrates them and what makes them want to do better.

▲ Psychology: Helps us to understand people. Inherently, the vast majority of us come to work wanting to do our best, already motivated. Effective organisations engage that motivation, others dampen it. Furthermore, we think, learn and communicate in different ways and at different speeds. We are all different. Good management helps us to nurture and preserve the diverse innate attributes of people.

HOW SOME DEFINITIONS DON'T HELP

A dinna ken fit wye ower mony folk mak a richt cuddy o a fyow wee ideas. They're sae ill-defined aat hale screeds hiv been scrievit fir business aat jist dinna mak ony sense.

I don't know how so many people make a real mess of a few small ideas. They are so badly defined that whole articles have been written for business that just don't make any sense.

▲ It is quite remarkable how the definition, interpretation and use of four apparently simple terms can be confused in such a way that entire international business standards, alleged 'best practice' guidance and the basis of management system design can be compromised and rendered worse than useless for many organisations.

A'm spikkin aboot:
- *the wye ti dee things*
- *thingies aat are pit in*
- *fit happens fan thingies are sae chyngit aboot aat they're nae the same fan they kim oot the ither end*
- *thingies aat are pit oot or kim oot.*

A'm fair flummoxed at the wye some folk conter fit they spik in ae breath fan they open their moos jist a minutie doon the road.
- I am talking about:
  - processes
  - inputs
  - transformations
  - outputs.

I am really at a loss to understand the way in which some people contradict what they say in one breath when they open their mouths just a minute later.

▲ The terms in question are:
  ▲ process
  ▲ input
  ▲ transformation
  ▲ product.

When some people try to explain their definitions, they confuse rather than assist

An wid ye nae expeck fowk fa read aa ess styte ti say, 'Jist hing oan a minutie – ess is aa jist sae muckle haivers!'? Bit it's aa got sae oot o haun noo aat an affa lot o yon heid bummer chiels are blin ti fit's gyaan oan.

And would you not expect people who read this rubbish to say, 'Wait a moment – this is all just so much claptrap!'? But it has all got so out of hand now that a

significant proportion of managers are blind to what is
going on.

▲ What is even more astounding is that some of the
definitions, explanations and usage are so blatantly
contradictory that you would expect any reader to
challenge them – but the entire approach to business
process management has now been so radically
comprised that it is difficult if not impossible for
many managers even to recognise the problem.

*The aal-farrant defineetion o 'the wye ti dee things' is
'a bourachie o things ti dee aat aa haud thegither sae
aat the thingies aat ging in are chyngit aboot ti mak
ither thingies aat are pit oot'.*
The traditional definition of 'how to do things' is 'a
collection of things to do which all hold together so
that things which go in are changed to create other
things which are put out'.

▲ The 'traditional' definition of a process is 'a set of
interrelated or interacting activities which transforms
inputs into outputs'.

*Some gypes ging oan an say aat 'the thingies aat ging
in are fit ye need ti be able ti dee aa ess – like ingines,
sillar, fowkies . . .' There's nae a business gyaan aboot
aat's efter chyngin aboot its ain folk finivver they lift a
finger ti dee onythin. Fit they're oan aboot is 'handy
things ti hae handy' sae aat the wark gits deen.*
Some people with a less than perfect reasoning ability
go on to say that 'the things which go in are what you
need too be able to do all this – such as engines,
money, people . . .' There isn't a business in existence
whose aim is to change its staff every time they lift a
finger to do anything. What they mean is the 'resources'
needed to get work done.

▲ Inputs are the things that we need in order to be able to carry out these activities – for example, equipment, finance, people. . . . Are there really organisations which transform their staff and computer systems? These are resources – the things that we need in order to . . .

WHAT IS A PROCESS?

Processes are aawye in business – bit maist fowk hiv an affa job ti spot een, nivver myn ti spell oot fit it is. Jist like yon ISO 9000 jing a ring, processes dinna jist bide in a mull. Business and processes are aa inaboot een anither – gin ye ken yer processes then ye'll ken yer business an aa.

Although processes are at the heart of business operations, many people find great difficulty in recognising a process, let alone in defining one. Business processes, like quality standards, are not confined to a mill, factory or production line. Business and processes are essentially interlinked – understand your processes and you will understand your business too.

The aal-farrant definishun o a process is aa ti dee wi a conveyor belt, mair's the peety. Mair general processes need a definishun aat's mair ti dee wi fit fowk dee in ither seetivations an aat kin aften be ti munnage an hunnle a fyowe shotties o a pucklie o processes in ae day.

Unfortunately, the traditional definition of a process derives from a manufacturing/continuous production process viewpoint. More general business processes need a definition that reflects what people do in other situations, which can often be to manage and act

[50]

within multiple instances of different processes within a working day.

Maist times, a process will affeck fowk in a pucklie o bourachies. Bumf an stuff'll ging fae ae bourachie ti the neist – an aat's faur there's a fair chunce aat there micht be a bit o guddle.

Fir fowk oan their ain, makin up yer myn an bletherin are processes an aa. Maist times, fowk spik fir a rizzon an there's aye a pucklie things aat kin mak a difference ti foo weel ye kin git the message ower.

Typically a process will involve people in more than one functional department. Information and/or material will pass from one department to the next – with the associated risk of misunderstanding or lack of communication at the interface. Some examples of business processes are:

- recruiting a new member of staff
- maintaining a piece of equipment
- carrying out a risk assessment.

At a personal level, a process is involved when you:

make a decision

old a conversation

Even making a statement is a process there will be an objective (to give information) and there will be a number of factors which influence how well the message is transmitted and received.

A've hird o a pucklie chiels fas mithers-in-laa spik sae muckle aat they nivver git ti the end o a sintince – the wifie's awa on ti the neist an the last een's nae half deen. Sae fit ti dee? Div ye feenish ilka sintince in yer ain heid or div ye hing on til aa the bitties o aa the sintinces, gie them a rummle aboot fan she staps fir air an syne mak up yer ain endins? A'm richt glad A'm nae een o thon chiels!

I have heard of some men whose mothers-in-law never get to the end of a sentence – they are away on to the next one and the last one is not half finished. So what do you do? Do you finish each sentence in your own head or do you hang on to all the pieces of all the partial sentences, mix them about when she stops for breath and then make up your own endings? I am so pleased that I am not one of those!

The wye ye spik fair maks a difference tee. Some fowk git richt cairrit awa wi excitemint fan they spik. A myn yon grumphie fairmer turned oily mannie Max ('nae sense ti the rest o us') Proctor, aifter twa-three (or mebbe it wis mair) pynts aifter a game o rugby – we aye hid ti tell him, 'Jist spit it oot, Maxie – we'll read fit yer sayin aff the wa!'

The way you speak makes a significant difference as well. Some people get totally carried away with excitement when they speak. I remember the pig farmer turned oil industry professional Max ('no sense to the rest of us') Proctor, after a few pints after a game of rugby – we always had to tell him, 'Just spit it out Maxie – we will read what you are saying off the wall!'

Sae the lesson fae aa aat is aat there's aften mair nor ae wye ti git ti faur ye're needin ti ging – dinna ging ramstam intilt athoot haein a thochtie aboot fit'll wark best.

So the lesson from all this is that there's often more than one way to get to where you want to get to – don't rush into it without thinking about what will work best.

WHAT WAS WRONG WITH THE OLD WAYS?

Traditional structures

An affa lot of fowk are aye wirkin in bourachies wi a heid bummer in each. Fan ess happins, fowk kin spend mair time thinking aboot fit wye ti mak their ain heid bummer chufft an they foryet aa aboot ither fowk. Fowk winna dee onythin aat's nae spellt oot an, if somebody maks a cuddy o somethin, there's aye fowk ready ti pynt the finger. There's an affa time spint scrievin lang stories aboot fit wye ti dee things, rither an makin't easy fir fowk jist ti git oan an dee the job.

Many people still work in groups with a manager in each. When this happens, people can spend more time thinking about how to please their own manager that they forget all about other people. People won't do anything that is not spelled out and, if somebody makes a mess of something, there are always people ready to point the finger. There is much time spent writing long stories about how to do things, rather than making it easy for people just to get on and do the job.

▲ Many organisations still have a traditional departmental and line management structure, which often results in an inward-looking working environment. This emphasises the control of procedures (and staff), demarcation of roles and a 'blame' culture, in which customer needs are sometimes forgotten. Manuals are often produced to satisfy an external requirement rather than to help staff do their job better. Such a structure tends to support and re-enforce a 'command and control' attitude. Senior managers tell managers what to do and they in turn tell the supervisors what to do and so on down the line. If something unusual happens, then you ask your superior how to handle it. Under no circumstances do you use your initiative. And, if something goes wrong, then the initial reaction is to blame someone.

An fowk hae muckle buiks aat spell oot fit aabody shid dee. Fit's waur, they hiv ae buik fir 'Quality', anither fir 'The Environment', anither fir 'Health an Safety' – an neen o them gies ye ony idea o fit wye the business acktually gings aboot getting the job deen.

And people have big books which spell out what everybody should do. What is worse, they have one book for 'Quality', another for the 'The Environment', another for 'Health and Safety' – and none of them gives you any idea of how the business actually goes about getting the job done.

▲ The 'traditional' way to define how a business does (or should) operate is to define a set of 'procedures', narrative descriptions of related sequences of events within a department or work area (for example, in Stores or Purchasing). Often, a company will generate one set of procedures for its quality system, another for how it deals with environmental matters and another for how it addresses heath and safety issues.

Narrative

Fan ye spell aathin oot in wirds, fit happins is:
- *there's nae jist ae wye ti cry fit somebody dis or fit ae bit o bumf is caad*
- *it's easy ti say fit shid be deen bit it's jist as easy nae ti say fa shid dee't*
- *foo mony wyes kin ye say the same thing?*

- *ae pucklie wirds kin conter ither eens bit ye canna spot it aat easy an ilka pucklie wirds kin soun fair convincin bit they jist dinna hing thegither*
- *gin it's aa a bittie o a rummle ti stert wi, some fowk blether oan a bittie mair an it aa jist gits waur.*

Nae winner aat fowk shak their heids, mak their shooders ging aa humphie an jist git oan wi it.

When you spell everything out in words, what happens is:

- there's not just one way to describe what somebody does or what a document is called
- it's easy to say what is to be dome but it is just as easy not to say who should do it
- how many ways can you say the same thing?
- a few words can contradict other ones but you can't spot it that easily, and each few words can sound really convincing, but they just don't hang together

If it is all a bit disorganised to start with, some people add more words and it just gets worse. No wonder people shake their heads, shrug their shoulders and just get on with it.

▲ Typical problems with the narrative procedures found in many organisations are:
  ▲ inconsistent terminology – the same job function or document may be referred to by a number of different names
  ▲ the responsibility for taking action is not clear
  ▲ repetition – the same instructions may appear (in slightly different wording) in different sections of a procedure
  ▲ there can be contradictions from one part of a procedure to another and there can be gaps where it is not clear how an action is supposed to follow from an earlier step

[55]

▲ a tendency to add more words to 'explain'
something which is not clear, thus making the
problem worse

Because such procedures can be difficult to understand,
they tend not to be used and sit on shelves where they
become out of date.

Fit ti jouk sae aat ye dee't better:
- *Dinna blether oan*
- *Expeck aat things'll ging richt maist o the time*
- *Myn fit wye ye're deein things i the first place*
- *Nae openin yer een wide eneuch*
- *Nae seein the moyens*
- *Being feart ti hae a richt go at the hale jing bang*

What to avoid so that you do it better:
- Don't ramble
- Expect that things will go right most of the time
- Remember why you are doing things in the first place
- Not opening your eyes wide enough
- Not seeing the influences
- Being afraid to have a real go at things.

▲ Common failings
  ▲ Too much detail
  ▲ Not focussing on the 'normal' path
  ▲ Lose sight of objectives
  ▲ Not seeing a process as 'generic'
  ▲ Not managing the Influences
  ▲ Not being radical enough!

HOW TO DESIGN A MANAGEMENT SYSTEM

GET THE STRUCTURE RIGHT

Aye set tee fae the tap – ye're spikkin aboot the wye the hale jing bang hings thegither

Always get going from the top – you are speaking about how everything hangs together.

▲ ALWAYS start at the top level and work down – 'running the business' is a process.

Nae mair nor sax ti echt bourachs – sic as:

● *Decidin Faur Ye're Gyaan an Giein Aathin a Gweed Redd Up*
● *Chappin Oan Doors*
● *Makin an Sellin Things*
● *Owerseein Aathin Ye Need Ti Hae Ti Haun*
● *Haein Anither Thochtie An Giein Onythin aat Needs it a Bittie Redd Up.*

No more than six to eight groups – such as:

● Having a Think and Giving Everything a Good Tidy Up
● Knocking on Doors
● Making and Selling Things
● Overseeing the Things and the People you Need to Help
● Having Another Think and Giving Anything that Needs it a Bit of a Tidy Up.

▲ Define no more than 6–8 top-level process groups – for example:
  ▲ Planning and Organising
  ▲ Getting and Doing Work
  ▲ Managing Resources
  ▲ Managing People
  ▲ Reviewing and Improving

Dinna get ower funcy wi yer nummers – ony gype kens aat fower cams efter three an, gin ye hae een caad '3–01–1', it's mair nor likely aat it's pairt o '3–01'.

Don't get over fancy with your numbering – any daftie knows that 4 comes after 3 and, if you have one called '3–01–1', it is more than likely that it is part of '3–01'.

▲ Use a simple numbering system for Processes to show the sequence and relationship of Processes and Sub-Processes within the Process Groups.

DEFINE A PROCESS

Mak richt sure aat ye ken fit wye ye're spellin oot the wye ti dee things – fa will mak eese o yer definition an fir fit?

Make really sure that you know why you are spelling out the way to do things – who will make use of the definition and for what?

▲ Be clear why you are defining the process – who will use the definition and for what?

Dinna git cairrit awa – ye dinna need ti scrieve a buik. Ye maun pit the message ower ti ony reader i the time it taks fae flypin yer socks ti pittin oan yer sheen. Fowk shid git the gist o things in less nor a meenit. Dinna waste a lot o bumf.

Don't get carried away – you don't need to write a book. You need to get the message over to any reader in the time it takes from turning your socks inside out to putting on your shoes. People should get the main points in less than a minute. Don't waste a lot of paper.

▲ Get the level of detail right – a reader should be able to scan and understand a process definition in, say, 30 seconds. This means no more than 2–3 pages of A4.

Tak it aat the fowk fa'll read yer spikk ken fit they're aboot – gin they're nae, it's up ti ye ti git them learnit.

Take it that the people who will read your definitions know what they are about – if they are not, it is up to you to get them taught.

▲ Assume competence in the user – if they are not competent, train them.

Dinna ficher aboot – mak up yer ain rowles an wye ti dee things an haud them on.

Don't fiddle about – make up your own rules and apply them consistently.

▲ Be consistent – apply a few basic standards and simple conventions and stick to them.

Picters work jist fine.

Pictures work very well.

▲ Use a graphical presentation – a simple diagram, such as a Deployment (Matrix) Flowchart, is ideal.

Myn aat ye maun dee mair nor jist draain a picter – hae a thochtie aboot the bumf ye maun mak up or hae a lookie at, fit ye need ti hae handy an onythin else aat kin hae a haun in the wye things wirk oot.

Remember that you must do more than just drawing a picture – have a think about documents you must create or refer to, what you need to have to hand and anything else that can help in the way things work out.

▲ Remember that a process definition is not (just) a Flowchart – also consider Reference Documents and Records/Resource Requirements/Influences.

DEFINE A TASK

Dinna blether – say fit's deen (lik 'Ca the hunnle', 'Dicht yer nib', 'Skelp his dock'). Ye kin aye add a fyowe mair wirds ti spell oot fit wye ti dee't gin fowk mebbe winna be richt sure.

Don't ramble on – say what is done (such as 'Turn the handle', 'Wipe your nose', 'Wallop his backside'). You can always add some explanation to spell out which way to do it if people maybe would not be completely certain.

▲ Be concise – use active verb/noun format. Use additional description if necessary to say how it is done.

Say fa dis fit – nae the fowks' names bit fit they dee. Nae mair than ae billie ti dee ae jobbie bit other fowk kin hae a haun in't an aa. Dinna git cairrit awa wi funcy picters.

Say who does what – not the people's names but what they do. No more than one person to do one task but other people can help with it as well. Don't get carried away with complicated pictures.

▲ Identify who is involved – Job Functions, not individuals. Only one responsible per task. Others may assist (perhaps as delegates), be consulted and be informed. Use a small number of symbols to identify the type of involvement.

Spell oot fit's aye deen. Haud on doon the page – gin ye ging across, ye'll get in a richt fankle fan ye reach the side.

Spell out what is normally done. Always go down the page – if you go across, you will get in a tangle when you reach the edge.

▲ Show the Normal Flow – a Vertical Presentation works best.

Dinna dee 'diamonds' – or nae gin ye kin help't. Ye kin aften pit yer 'fit ifs' intil the wirds.

Don't do 'diamonds' (i.e. flowcharting 'decision' symbols) – at least not if you can help it. You can often put your 'what ifs' into the task description.

▲ If possible, avoid decisions – or rather avoid Decision Symbols, Branches and Loop-Backs on Flowcharts. It is usually possible to word a task so that the 'Condition' is built into the task.

MANAGEMENT LESSONS

Lesson Number One

A craa wis sittin on a tree, deein nithin aa day. A wee rubbit spied the craa and spiered til him, 'Kin A sit on ma doup lik you an dee nithin aa day an aa?' The craa answered, 'Aye, fairly min, nae problem.' So, the rubbit parkit hissel on the grun aneth the craa an closed his een. Oot o the blue, a fox cam in aboot, loupit on the rubbit an swallaad him.

A crow was sitting on a tree, doing nothing all day. A small rabbit saw the crow and asked him, 'Can I also sit like you and do nothing all day long?' The crow answered, 'Certainly, why not?' So, the rabbit sat on the ground below the crow and rested. All of a sudden, a fox appeared, jumped on the rabbit and ate him.

Management Lesson

If ye're gyaan ti sit on yer erse aa day an dee nithin, ye'd best be affa hich.

To be sitting doing nothing, you must be sitting very, very high up.

Lesson Number Two

A bubblyjock wis bletherin til a bull. 'A wid fair funcy fleein up ti the tap o yon tree,' soochit the bubblyjock, 'bit A've nae fooshun.' 'Ye cwid aye hae a chaav on fit A've drappit ahin me,' said the bull. 'It'll fairly gie ye a hairy bosie'.

The bubblyjock aet a pucklie lumps of the sharn an – fair doos – he wis able ti flee up til the first brench. The neist day, aifter chaan mair sharn, he wis up til the seekint brench. Feenally, aifter a full twa wikks, he thocht he wis Airchie, cockit on the verra heid of the tree.

In nae time ava, a fairmer chiel spied him an pluffit a bullit intil his heid.

A turkey was chatting with a bull. 'I would love to be able to get to the top of that tree,' sighed the turkey, 'but I haven't got the energy.' 'Well, why don't you nibble on some of my droppings?' replied the bull. 'They're packed with nutrients.'

The turkey pecked at a lump of dung and found that it actually gave him enough strength to reach the first branch of the tree. The next day, after eating some more dung, he reached the second branch. Finally, after a fortnight, there he was proudly perched at the top of the tree. He was promptly spotted by a farmer who fired a bullet into his head.

Management Lesson

Sharn fae a bull will mebbe git ye ti the tap, but it winnae keep ye there.

Bullshit might get you to the top, but it won't keep you there.

Lesson Number Three

A wee burdie wis fleein sooth fir the winter. It wis sae caul, the burdie turnit til ice an drappit ti the grun in a muckle park. Fan it wis leein there, a coo cam in aboot an drappit sharn ower the heid o't. As the burdie wis happit i sharn, it hid a thochtie aboot fou warm it wis. It wis aat chuffit aboot it aat he seen set tee geein it laldie wie his singin. Jist then, a moggie luggit intae the stushie an cam in aboot ti hae a spy. It gaed richt in aboot, caad the sharn ti ae side, loupit on the burdie an swallit it.

A little bird was flying south for the winter. It was so cold, the bird froze and fell to the ground in a large field. While it was lying there, a cow came by and dropped some dung on it. As the frozen bird lay there in the pile of cow dung, it began to realise how warm it was. The dung was actually thawing him out! He lay there all warm and happy and soon began to sing for joy. A passing cat heard the bird singing and came to investigate. Following the sound, the cat discovered the bird under the pile of cow dung and promptly dug him out and ate him.

Management Lessons

1 Nae aabody fa cacks oan yer heid is agin ye.

Not everyone who drops shit on you is your enemy.

2 Nae aabody fa gies ye a haun ti git oot the sharn is yer chum.

Not everyone who gets you out of shit is your friend.

3 Fan ye're up ti yer oxters in sharn, haud yer wheesht.

When you're in deep shit, keep your mouth shut.

Lesson Number Four

A chiel wis fleein aboot in a het-air balloon fan he hid a richt fleg cos he hid nae idea o faur he wis. He gings doon a bittie an spies a mannie in a park. He gings doon a bittie farrer an speirs, 'Aye, aye, min, kin ye tell me faur A am?'

The mannie says, 'Aye, fairly aat – ye're in a het-air balloon, hingin aboot 30 fit abune ess park.'

'Div ye wirk in IT?' speirs the mannie in the balloon.

'Aye, A div aat,' the mannie replies. 'An fit wye div ye ken aat?'

'Weel, weel' says the balloonist, 'fit ye telt wis the trowth but it wis nae muckle eese til man nor beast'.

The mannie doon below says, 'Ye're nae een o thae heid bummer fowk, are ye?'

'Aat's richt,' says the chiel in the balloon, 'fit wye did ye ken?'

'Weel', says the mannie, 'ye dinna ken faur ye are or faur ye're gyaan bit ye expeck me ti gie ye a haun. Ye're nae farrer oan nor afore we met bit noo it's aa ma blame!'

A man piloting a hot air balloon discovers he has wandered off course and is hopelessly lost. He descends to a lower altitude and locates a man down on the ground. He lowers the balloon further and shouts 'Excuse me, can you tell me where I am?'

The man below says, 'Yes, you're in a hot air balloon, about 30 feet above this field.'

'You must work in Information Technology,' says the balloonist.

'Yes I do,' replies the man. 'And how did you know that?'

'Well,' says the balloonist, 'what you told me is technically correct but of no use to anyone.'

The man below says, 'You must work in management.'

'I do,' replies the balloonist, 'how did you know?'

'Well,' says the man, 'you don't know where you are or where you're going but you expect my immediate help. You're in the same position you were before we met but now it's all my fault!'

LEADERSHIP TIPS

Jack Welch the business leader and writer, formerly of General Electric, is quoted as proposing these fundamental leadership principles:

There's nocht bit ae wye ti dee things – dinna be sleekit. Gin ye dee aat, ither fowk will like as not dee the same. There is but one way to do things – don't be sly. If you do that, other people are more than likely to act in the same way.

▲ There is only one way – the straight way. It sets the tone of the organisation.

Sik oot fit's braw. Mak siccar aat aabody gits ti ken. Seek out what is good. Make sure that everyone gets to know.

▲ Be open to the best of what everyone, everywhere, has to offer. Transfer learning across your organisation.

Pit the richt fowk ti dee the richt jobbies – it maks mair sense nor haein a funcy palaver fir faur ye're gyaan.

[65]

Put the right people to do the right jobs – it makes more sense than having a complex strategy.

▲ Get the right people in the right jobs – it is more important than developing a strategy.

Dinna be ower stuffy.
Don't be pompous.

▲ An informal atmosphere is a competitive advantage.

Mak siccar aat aabody maiters – an aat they aa ken fine aat's the wye o't.
Make sure that everyone matters – and that they all know clearly that is how things are.

▲ Make sure everybody counts and everybody knows they count.

Haein a guid conceit o yersel is fine – dinna be feart ti spik oot.
Having a good opinion of yourself is fine – do not be afraid to speak out.

▲ Legitimate self-confidence is a winner – the true test of self-confidence is the courage to be open.

Hae a lauch
Have a laugh.

▲ Business has to be fun – celebrations energise an organisation.

Ther's aye a chunce aat ither fowk micht dee fit ye dinna expeck.
There is always a chance that other people might do what you do not expect.

▲ Never underestimate the other guy.

Git yer heid roon fit really coonts an pit yer tap fowk in aboot.

Get your head around what really counts and put your top people into it.

▲ Understand where real value is added and put your best people there.

Ken fan ti ficher aboot an fan ti haud back – yer heid'll tell ye.

Know when to tinker and when to hold back – your head will tell you.

▲ Know when to meddle and when to let go – this is pure instinct.

Gin ye're the heid bummer, ye maun caa awa till the jobbie's deen. Ken faur ye're gyaan an fit wye ye'll git there. Git yer fowk aa workin thegither an giein aabody else a haun. Ken yersel an aa. Pit a team thegither an divvy up the wirk. An, gin onybody maks a richt cuddy o somethin, dinna baal them oot.

If you are the boss, you must keep at it until the project is complete. Know where you are going and which way you will get there. Get your people all working together and helping each other. Know yourself as well. Put a team together and divide the work. And, if anybody makes a real mess of something, do not give them a public dressing down.

▲ As a leader, your main priority is to get the job done. Leaders make things happen by:
  ▲ knowing their objectives and having a plan how to achieve them
  ▲ building a team committed to achieving the objectives
  ▲ helping each team member to give their best efforts.

Know your own strengths and weaknesses, so that you can build the best team around you. Keep the right balance between 'doing' yourself and managing others. Take the blame and accept responsibility for any failings or mistakes that your people make. Never publicly blame another person for a failing.

LEARNING LESSONS

Haein a rake aboot ti see fit wint rang
Investigating the cause of an accident

Aifter a mishanter fan somebody maks a cuddy o things, fowk dinna aawyes pit eneuch effort intil unnerstannin aa the rizzons. Bit, gin ye dinna hae a gweed rake aboot, there's a fair chunce aat nithin will chynge.

After an accident involving human failure there may be an investigation into the causes and contributing factors. Very often, little attempt is made to understand why the human failures occurred. However, finding out both the immediate and the underlying causes of an accident is the key to preventing similar accidents through the design of effective control measures.

It's thingies lik:
Ti dee wi the job:
- *gypit design o the wye the biggin is riggit oot*
- *a carfuffle's gyaan oan aa the time*
- *fowk dinna ken fit ti dee*
- *ingines are gyaan roostie*
- *ower muckle ti dee*
- *an affa racket an the hale place is mingin.*

It's things like:
Job-related:
- thoughtless design of the way the building is equipped
- disorder going on all the time
- people don't know what to do
- engines are becoming rusty
- too much to do
- an awful noise and the whole place is very dirty.

▲ Typical examples of immediate causes and contributing factors for human failures are:
Job factors:
   ▲ illogical design of equipment and instruments
   ▲ constant disturbances and interruptions
   ▲ missing or unclear instructions
   ▲ poorly maintained equipment
   ▲ high workload
   ▲ noisy and unpleasant working conditions

Ti dee wi the fowk deein the job:
- *jist fit fir orra jobbies*
- *fair forfochen*
- *scunnert or dischuffed*
- *nae weel*

Personnel-related:
- just fit for odd jobs
- really tired
- fed up or unhappy
- not well

▲ Individual factors:
   ▲ low skill and competence levels
   ▲ tiredness
   ▲ boredom or disheartened staff
   ▲ individual medical problems.

[69]

Ti dee wi the wye aathin hauds thegither:
- *ower muckle ti dee sae aat fowk git hasht*
- *nivver a gaird fan ye need een*
- *nithin chynges*
- *heid bummers aa spik, bit their lugs are nae switched oan*
- *aabody's aa ower the place*
- *naebody's aat fussit gin ye mischieve yersel.*

Organisational matters:
- too much to do so that people get harassed
- never a guard when you need one
- nothing changes
- managers all talk but their ears are not receptive
- everyone is disorganised
- no one is too bothered if you hurt yourself.

▲ Organisation and management factors:
   ▲ poor work planning, leading to high work pressure
   ▲ lack of safety systems and barriers
   ▲ inadequate responses to previous incidents
   ▲ management based on one-way communications
   ▲ deficient co-ordination and responsibilities
   ▲ poor management of health and safety
   ▲ poor health and safety culture.

HUMAN ERROR

A human error is when an action or decision was not intended and this involved a deviation from an accepted standard and led to an undesirable outcome. A violation is a deliberate deviation from a rule or procedure. Errors fall into three categories: slips, lapses and mistakes. Slips and lapses occur in very familiar tasks which we can carry out without much need for conscious attention.

Slips

Makkin a cuddy o't kin mean:
- *deein somethin ower early or ower late*
- *nae deein it ava*
- *bein a bittie roch wi't or a bittie saft*
- *gyaan the wrang wye*
- *deein it richt bit nae ti the richt thing*
- *deeing the wrang thing ti the richt thing.*

Making a mess of something can mean:
- doing something too early or too late
- not doing it all
- being a bit rough with it or a bit soft
- going the wrong way
- doing it correctly but not to the right thing
- doing the wrong thing to the right thing.

▲ Slips are failures in carrying out the actions of a task. Typical slips might include:
  ▲ performing an action too soon in a procedure or leaving it too late
  ▲ omitting a step or series of steps from a task
  ▲ carrying out an action with too much or too little strength
  ▲ performing the action in the wrong direction
  ▲ doing the right thing but on the wrong object (e.g. switching the wrong switch)
  ▲ carrying out the wrong check but on the right item (e.g. checking a dial but for the wrong value).

Lapses

A 'lapse' is nae myndin ti dee somethin ava. It's nae eese gin fowk hiv ti thole a stramash – mak it easy fir them ti haud til the job. Mebbe ye cwid gie the hale jing bang a gweed redd up.

A 'lapse' is not remembering to do something at all. It
is no use if people have to put up with a commotion –
make it easy for them to stick to the job. Perhaps you
could give the whole set-up a good tidy.

▲ Lapses cause us to forget to carry out an action, to
lose our place in a task or even to forget what we
had intended to do. They can be reduced by
minimising distractions and interruptions to tasks
and by providing effective reminders especially for
tasks which take some time to complete or involve
periods of waiting. A useful reminder could be as
simple as a partially completed checklist placed
in a clearly visible location for the person doing
the task. We may be able to eliminate some of
these lapses through better design of equipment
or tasks.

Mistakes

*A 'mistack' his a bittie mair tee't – it's fan we dee the
wrang thing bit think it's richt. Ae kin o mistack is fan
we try ti fit fit we hae ti dee intil a wye of deein aat
fits anither seetivation aathegither.*

A 'mistake' has a bit more to it – it's when we do the
wrong thing but think it's right. One kind of mistake is
when we try to fit what we have to do into a way of
doing that fits another situation altogether.

▲ Mistakes are a more complex type of error where
we do the wrong thing believing it to be right.
Rule-based mistakes occur when our behaviour is
based on remembered rules or familiar procedures.
We have a strong tendency to use familiar rules or
solutions even when these are not the most
convenient or efficient.

Gin we're nae richt sure aboot fit wye ti ging, we'll hae ti mak't up on the hoof – an aat's nae ayewis aat easy.
If we are not completely sure about which way to go, we will have to make it up as we go – and that is not always that easy.

▲ In unfamiliar circumstances, we have to revert to consciously making goals, developing plans and procedures. Planning or problem solving needs us to reason from first principles or use analogies. Misdiagnoses and miscalculations can result when we use this knowledge-based reasoning.

Maistly it's skeely fowk fa mak is sort o mistack. Bit it's eyven waur fir fowk fa hivna deen't afore an fa dinna git telt eneuch aboot fits gyaan oan afore they git yokit thirsels.
Mostly it is skilled people who make this sort of mistake. But it is even worse for people who haven't done it before and who are not told enough about what is going on before they get started themselves.

▲ The kinds of error described above typically occur with people who are experienced and trained. It is important to remember that human errors often occur if a person is not experienced or does not receive the correct information such as knowledge of potential hazards. Lack of understanding often arises through a failure to communicate effectively. Shift handovers are a particularly vulnerable time for communication failures.

It's aa maist likely ti cam aboot gin:
- *there's an affa steer, it's ower het or yer heid's dirlin*
- *it's a sair fecht ti concentrate*
- *aabody's hashed – baith yersel an ither fowk*
- *aathin's in a bit o a snorl.*

It is all most likely to happen if:
- there is an awful commotion, its too hot or your head is ringing
- it's an effort (sore fight) to concentrate
- everybody is under pressure – both yourself and other people
- everything is rather confused and entangled.

▲ Errors are more likely to occur under certain circumstances, including:
  ▲ work environment stressors – e.g. extremes of heat, humidity, noise, vibration, poor lighting, restricted workspace
  ▲ extreme task demands – e.g. high workload, tasks demanding high levels of alertness, jobs which are very monotonous and repetitive, situations with many distractions and interruptions
  ▲ social and organisational stressors – e.g. insufficient staffing levels, inflexible or overdemanding work schedules, conflicts with work colleagues, peer pressure and conflicting attitudes to health and safety
  ▲ individual stressors – e.g. inadequate training and experience, high levels of fatigue, reduced alertness, family problems, ill-health, misuse of alcohol and drugs
  ▲ equipment stressors – e.g. poorly designed displays and controls, inaccurate and confusing instructions and procedures.

Sae fit ti dee?
So what to do?
Error control and reduction needs to consider the influences on peoples' behaviour and performance.

Hae a shottie at:
- *reddin up fit's gyaan oan roon aboot*
- *gittin aathin riggit oot proper*
- *gittin fowk learnit*
- *nae makkin the job ower fashous.*

Have a go at:
- sorting out what is going on round about
- getting everything fitted out properly
- giving people the skills and knowledge they need
- not making the job too troublesome.

▲ Steps to reduce human errors include:
  ▲ addressing the conditions and reducing the stressors which increase the frequency of errors
  ▲ designing plant and equipment to prevent slips and lapses occurring or to increase the chance of detecting and correcting them
  ▲ making certain that arrangements for training are effective
  ▲ designing jobs to avoid the need for tasks which involve very complex decisions, diagnoses or calculations – e.g. by writing procedures for rare events requiring decisions and actions.

Swickin the system
Breaking the rules

Swickin is fan ye canna say, 'A didna ken.' It's mair lik, 'Aye, aye, aat's aa verra weel bit A ken better.' It's nae aye aat fowk are ill-trickit bit mair aat they're hashin oan an dinna see the pint in aa thae rules. An, gin ither fowk git aff wi't an aa, fowk expeck aat aat's jist the wye o't.

Breaking the rules is when you can't say, 'I didn't know.' It's more like, 'Yes, yes, that's all very well but

I know better.' It's not always that people are mischievous but more that they're working under pressure and don't see the point in all those rules. And, if other people get away with it as well, people expect that that is just the way of it.

▲ Violations are any deliberate deviations from rules, procedures, instructions and regulations. The breaching or violating of health and safety rules or procedures is a significant cause of many accidents and injuries at work. Removing the guard on dangerous machinery or driving too fast will clearly increase the risk of an accident. Health risks are also increased by rule breaking.

▲ In the workplace rules are broken for many different reasons. Most violations are motivated by a desire to carry out the job despite the prevailing constraints, goals and expectations. Very rarely are they wilful acts of sabotage or vandalism. Violations are divided into three categories: routine, situational and exceptional.

▲ With a routine violation, breaking the rule or procedure has become a normal way of working within the work group. This can be due to:

  ▲ the desire to cut corners to save time and energy

  ▲ the perception that the rules are too restrictive

  ▲ the belief that the rules no longer apply

  ▲ lack of enforcement of the rule

  ▲ new workers starting a job where routine violations are the norm and not realising that this is not the correct way of working.

PROBLEMS CAUSED BY POOR PROCEDURES

Spellin oot fit ti dee, fit wye, an fa shid dee't
Procedures

> *Gin fowk canna mak oot fit they're supposed ti dee, ther's a fair chunce they winna dee't – nae guff.*

- *Kin fowk git their hauns oan fit they need?*
- *Div fowk eese't?*
- *Kin aabody git a hunnle oan fit it means?*
- *Dis't descrive fit fowk dee?*
- *Dis't help ti stop fowk mischievin thirsels?*
- *Fan dis't git a redd up?*

If people can't make out what they are supposed to do, there is a fair chance they won't do it – no unnecessary words.

- Can people get their hands on what they need?
- Do people use it?
- Can everyone get a grasp on what it means?
- Does it describe what people do?
- Does it help stop people hurting themselves?
- When does it get updated?

▲ Poor procedures and instructions can be a reason for people not following recommended actions. As well as being technically accurate, procedures need to be well-written, usable and up to date. Remember that even if your procedures are not formally written down they exist through the working practices of staff. Ask yourself:

▲ Are your procedures accessible?
▲ Are they actually followed by staff?
▲ Are they written so that they can be understood and followed easily?

[77]

▲ Do they reflect the tasks as they are actually carried out?
▲ Do the procedures include key safety information?
▲ Are they kept up to date and reviewed occasionally?

WRITING BETTER PROCEDURES

Hae a thochtie aboot:
- *Fa'll read em?*
- *Foo muckle help maun they hae?*
- *Fit wye'll they eese em – jist fan they git yokit ti the job or ilka time they lift a finger?*
- *If they need mair bumf, is't tae haun?*

Have a think about:
- Who will read them?
- How much help must they have?
- How will they use them – just when they get started on the job, or every time they left a finger?
- If they need more information, is it available?

▲ You will also need to have the results of any relevant risk assessments to hand so that the procedure can reflect arrangements to maintain adequate control of identified risks. So:
  ▲ consider both the difficulty and importance of the task(s) to be documented
  ▲ find out how often the task is carried out and the potential hazards
  ▲ think about who will use the procedure and the level of information they need (providing too much information may lead to less use of the procedure if users find it too detailed and hard to follow; offering too little information may mean

that an inexperienced person will not be able to carry out the task)

▲ establish the skills, experience level, past training and needs of the users of the procedure and look at whether the procedure needs to be supported by training in order to promote understanding and effective use

Fir ony job, hae a thochtie aboot:

- *Fa dis't?*
- *Fit div they dee?*
- *Fit div they need ti hae ti haun?*
- *Fit wye div they hae ti ging?*
- *Fit div they need ti ken?*
- *Faur dis ess com fae?*
- *Fit div they need ti ken ti caa awa an nae think twice?*
- *Foo aften dis it happin?*
- *Faur aboot dis it happin?*
- *Fit's gyaan oan roon aboot fan it's happinin?*
- *Div they need ti hash oan?*
- *Kin onythin cowp, git in a snorl or git aa rummlt aboot?*
- *Fa micht be mischievit?*

For any job have a think about:

- Who does it?
- What do they do?
- What do they need to have to hand?
- Which direction do they have to go?
- What do they need to know?
- Where does this come from?
- What do they need to know to work away and not think twice?
- How often does it happen?
- Where about does it happen?

- What is going on roundabout when it is happening?
- Do they need to work quickly?
- Can anything overturn, get in a tangle to get put in a stat of disorder?
- Who might be injured?

▲ It is often helpful to look at a particular job, task or activity in a given work setting. So think about:
  ▲ Who does this activity?
  ▲ Exactly what tasks/action do they do?
  ▲ What tools or equipment are needed?
  ▲ What decisions are made?
  ▲ What information is needed to do the task?
  ▲ Where does this information come from (people/paper/computers/displays)?
  ▲ How is the task learned and competence assessed?
  ▲ How often is the activity carried out?
  ▲ Where is the task carried out?
  ▲ What is the working environment like (temperature/noise/lighting/etc.)?
  ▲ Are there time constraints on the task?
  ▲ What can go wrong? Where is there potential to make errors?
  ▲ How can failures be detected and corrected?
  ▲ What health and safety consequences can result?

EDDIE'S SAX THINKIN BUNNETS

De Bono's Six Thinking Hats

Edward de Bono is regarded as the leading authority in the world in the field of creative thinking and is the originator of lateral thinking. His 'Six Thinking Hats' methodology shows how to separate your thinking into six distinct modes. Each mode is identified with a different coloured 'thinking hat'. By mentally donning and switching 'Hats' you can focus or redirect your thought.

THE FITE BUNNET
Fit ye ken. Fit ye need ti ken.

THE WHITE HAT
What you know. What you need to know.
▲ WHITE HAT THINKING
▲ Information available and needed.
▲ Facts: Identifying and communicating all of the relevant data and facts, to gather the necessary missing data for any project, problem, decision, concern or opportunity in order to arrive at a sound conclusion.

THE YALLA BUNNET
Fit wye it micht wirk.

THE YELLOW HAT
Which way it might work.
▲ YELLOW HAT THINKING
▲ Values and benefits – why something might work
▲ Positive Value: Identifying and finding the value, feasibility and benefits in ideas, proposals, suggestions or potential solutions. A mind shift from the idea-killer habit of knocking ideas down as soon as they are suggested.

THE BLAIK BUNNET
Aye aye, aat's aa verra weel, bit A'm nae richt sure aat . . .

THE BLACK HAT
Yes, yes, that's all very well, but I'm not really sure that . . .

[81]

▲ BLACK HAT THINKING
▲ Cautions and difficulties – where things might go wrong.
▲ Difficulties: Identifying all of the logical reasons why something might not work. To use this valuable information to design a project plan that will eliminate the faults before taking action. Ensuring success.

THE GREEN BUNNET
Fit aboot is an fit aboot aat an fit jist micht tak a trick?

THE GREEN HAT
What about this and what about that and what might just take a trick?
▲ GREEN HAT THINKING
▲ Alternatives and creative ideas.
▲ Creative Thinking: Generating ideas, possibilities and alternatives. Expanding your options – the world of the possible. Generating ideas that will overcome the difficulties pointed out in Black Hat Thinking. Designing your way into the future.

THE REID BUNNET
Jist mebbe . . .

THE RED HAT
Just perhaps . . .
▲ RED HAT THINKING
▲ Intuition, feelings and hunches.
▲ Intuition: Communicating your hunches, gut instincts or feelings about a subject. It also enables the mind to move beyond initial reactions and get down to the productive business of exploring a subject much more thoroughly.

THE BLAE BUNNET
Mak sure aat aa the options git a fair shottie.

THE BLUE HAT
Ensure that all the options get a fair opportunity.
▲ BLUE HAT THINKING
▲ Managing the thinking process.
▲ Process Control: Thinking about your thinking before doing your thinking. Managing the thinking process. Creating thinking plans that will cover the appropriate thinking bases in order to achieve your desired end result.

5S

'5S' is a tool of Japanese origins that is used to provide a standard workplace environment, enabling standardised work and helping to remove waste. 5S involves employees maintaining an organised, efficient, safe and clean workplace. The philosophy behind 5S is – order, organisation, discipline, elimination of bad habits and wasted effort.

> *Sair ee? There's nithin lik a gweed redd oot if aathin is in a richt rummle – an if ye're nae richt sure aboot ae thing, pit it awa in the press wi a ticketie on't sae aat ither fowk kin find it fan they need it.*

That which is offensive to the eye? There is nothing like a good clear out if everything is in a real muddle – and if you are not too sure about one thing, put it in the cupboard with a label on it so that other people can find it when they need it

▲ Instant disposal of unnecessary things, arrangement or reorganisation. Clearout and classify, bin what you don't need, free up space. If not sure, use a red

tag and ask, 'Who owns it?' 'Can we bin it?' Store
other things not needed.

▲ <u>Seiri</u> 'Say-ree' – 'Sort'

*Aul Nick hissel? Mak yer desk, office or press leuk lik
hivven, nae hell. Dinna mak fowk scutter aboot ti find
onythin – hae a thinkie aboot fa needs fit an fan an
mak't easy fir onybody ti git their hauns on't.*

The devil himself? Make your desk, office or storage
cupboard like heaven, not hell. Don't make people
waste time finding anything – think about who needs it
and when and make it easy for anyone to get their
hands on it.

▲ Put things in order – a place for everything and
everything in its place. Order what is remaining
according to frequency of use. Create a standard
layout – easy to see if everything is in its place.

▲ <u>Saiton</u> 'Say-ton' – 'Set in order'

*Fa says? Git yir flannel oot, gie aathin a pucklie ile an
mak siccar aat aathin's jist tickety-boo fan ye caa the
hunnle.*

Who says? Get your cloth out, oil everything and make
sure that everything is just right when you wind it up
for use

▲ Clean to original condition, do clean work
positively. Clean and check. Ensure equipment is fit
for purpose.

▲ <u>Seiso</u> 'Says-oo' – 'Shine'

*(Fir Gaad's) Sake it's oo. A haimalt, naitral wye o deein
things.*

For goodness sake its wool. A down-to-earth, natural
way of working.

▲ Clean, pure, untainted workplace. Free from bad

habits. Conformity. Establish best way to do things
and format. Make this the standard and
communicate it.

▲ Seiketsu 'Say-kitsue' – Systemise, standardise

*Keechs fir Britain? Ging aboot things in a wye aat
maks ither fowk ken aat ye mean business. Aye
dee things the same wye an be sair ti please bit
weel-mennert.*

Craps for Britain? Go about things in a way which
makes other people know that you mean business.
Always do things the same way and be difficult to
please but well mannered.

▲ Be well mannered, use polite behaviour, be
disciplined. Maintain what has been achieved. Custom
and practice. Make it a habit and review frequently.

▲ Shitsuke 'Shit-zukay' – 'Sustain and Improve'

NEGATIVE ATTITUDES

'I don't 'do' such and such' is a particularly annoying modern
idiom. It does, however, lend itself to being combined with the
traditional north-east negativity – for example, *'nae bad'* means
'pretty good, really'.

A dinna:
I don't:

debar
A'm richt aff the drink the noo
I am teetotal at present

debrief
A'm a richt blether eence a git stairtit
I am a real gossip once I get going

decamp
> *Nae poncin aboot fir me*
> No fairying about for me

decease
> *A'm aat thrawn, it's nivver lowsin time fir me*
> I am so stubborn, it is never time for me to stop

deceit
> *A'll jist stan, thunks*
> I'll just stand, thanks

decide
> *A'm either richt oot at the front or roon the back*
> I am either right out at the front or round the back

decipher
> *A'm aye chaavin awa deein ae thing or anither*
> I am always working away doing one thing or another

declare
> *She's mairrit til ma best chum*
> She is married to my best friend

declassify
> *A skive aff skweel (gin A kin get aff wi't)*
> I play truant from school (if I can get off with it)

decompose
> *Ma lug's nae aat musical*
> My ear is not that tuneful

decoy
> *A'm affa bigsy, like*
> I'm rather full of myself

decreases
> *A even press ma semmit*
> I even iron my vest

decry
>*Nae if onybody's looking, onywye*
>
> Not if anyone is looking anyway

defame
>*A'm affa shy – real backirt at comin forrit*
>
> I am very shy – very backward at coming forward

default
>*A think A'm jist Airchie – gey near perfick*
>
> I think I am just the bee's knees – very near perfect

defeat
>*If ye're aifter haein yer taes pickit, it's Shand ye need*
>
> You will have to try the Ronnie Shand (Chiropody) Practice

defences
>*Mebbe aat's fit wye the beasts are aye aa ower the road*
>
> Maybe that's why the cattle are always all over the road

deferral
>*In fact, A'm fair domesticated*
>
> In fact, I am quite domesticated

defile
>*At's fit wye ma fingernails are a wee bittie roch*
>
> That is why my fingernails are slightly rough

deliberate
>*An wi aa the cutbacks wi the Scottish sodjers, A'm nae richt sure aat the airmy kin either*
>
> And with the cutback of the Scottish regiments, I am not convinced that the Army can either

deliver
>*Aa yon bluid maks me cowk*
>
> All that blood makes me retch

[87]

demean

> *An ye thocht aat an Aiberdonian disnae pit his haun in his pooch*
>
> And you thought that an Aberdonian doesn't put his hand in his pocket

demist

> *A'm aye spot on*
>
> I am always very accurate

demur

> *An A'm nae aat keen on frunkinsense or gold either*
>
> And I am not that keen on frankincense or gold either

denude

> *It's ower caul fir aat in Foggie*
>
> It's too cold for that in Aberchirder (known locally as Foggieloan)

depart

> *It's the hail jing bang or nithin ava*
>
> It's the whole lot or nothing at all

depict

> *A'm nae intil yon historical stuff*
>
> I am not into that historical stuff

deport

> *It gies me a sair heid nae handy*
>
> It gives me a sore head which is difficult to cope with

depose

> *Sae A widna fit in affa weel at yon funcy tearoom placie in Queens Road*
>
> So I would not feel comfortable in Café Society

depress

A git aa the news A can cope wi fae Grumpeen TV

I get all the news I can cope with from Grampian Television

derail

A need ti ken fan A'll arrive – ye canna aye rely oan fit Dickie Pickle tells ye

I need to know when I will arrive – you can't always rely on what Sir Richard Branson tells you

descend

If ye need it, get aff yer erse an come an git it yersel

If you need it, get off your backside and come and get it yourself

descent

OK, sae ma oxters are mebbe a bittie niffy

All right, so my armpits are perhaps a trifle odorous

describe

Since they shut maist o the Post Offices in toon, A dinna hae the time ti queue oot the door at Berryden ti buy a stump

Since the recent decimation of Post Office services in Aberdeen, I don't have the time to queue at the nearest Post Office I can find to buy a stamp

desire

A'm agin the monarchy or *Ma chubes hiv bin tied*

I am against the monarchy *or* I have had the operation

despair

We've bin doonsized sae A've ti unswer the phone an aathin

We have had another reduction in staff numbers so I have to answer the phone as well as everything else

despise
> *A leave aa aat ti MI5*
> I leave all that to MI5

detain
> *Beauly's ma limit – an it's a sair fecht ti mak it een aat far gin the win's agin us aa the wye fae Kintail*
> How adverse weather can affect performance in the Highland Cross

detest
> *A jist cross ma fingers an hope it'll be aa richt oan the nicht*
> I just cross my fingers and hope it will be all right on the night

devote
> *Thae politishuns is aa the same*
> Those politicians are all the same.

POSITIVE ATTITUDES (PERSONAL MASTERY)

> *Gin ye're aifter a chynge, chynge fit ye think o yersel first an lat the wye ye cairry on win tee wi the picter o yersel ye hae in yer heid.*
> If you want to change, change what you think of yourself first and let the way you behave catch up with the picture of yourself that you have in your head.
> ▲ If you want to change, change your self-image first and let your behaviour catch up with the new image.

> *Dinna jist sit back an lat things happen ti ye. Fit ye dee's in yer ain hauns.*
> Don't just sit back and let things happen to you. What you do is in your own hands.
> ▲ Make deliberate choices.

Haud yer haun up gin ye dinna dee aathing richt –
mak up a richt gweed picter o fit wye it will be fan ye
get yer neist shottie.

Admit it if you don't do everything right – make a really
good picture of the way it will be when you get your
next opportunity.

▲ Recognise where you fall short and imagine clearly
   how it should be the next time.

Hae a thinkie – fit gings oan in yer heid an fit wye div
ye dee things? Fit wye dis ess fit wi fit ye're aifter?

Think – what goes on in your head and how do you do
things? How does this fit with what you're seeking?

▲ Reflect – how do you think and act? Does this fit
   with what you want to achieve?

Fit div ye think athoot thinkin? Fit wye dis ess affeckt
fit wye ye see oangyaans an ither fowk?

What do you think without thinking? How does this
affect how you see happenings and other people?

▲ What do you believe? How do these beliefs affect
   how you see events and other people?

Fan ye've got yer heid roon fits in yer ain heid, ye'll
hae mair o a hunnle oan fit wye ither fowk are affeck-
tit bi the oangyaans in their ain heids.

When you have got your head round what is in your
own head, you'll have more of a grasp on how other
people are affected by the happenings in their own
heads.

▲ When you understand your own core beliefs, you
   will be able to understand more about how other
   people are affected by their beliefs.

Theres nae a richt definishun o 'reality'. Fit ye dee
fits wi fit's in yer heid. Sae fit ye dinna think aboot

affeckts fit wye ye see and think. Ye'll dee mair as ye chynge the wye ye see yersel an fit ye're fit fir.

There is not a correct definition of 'reality'. What you do matches what is in your head. So what you don't think about affects how you see and think. You'll do more as you change the way you see yourself and what you are capable of.

▲ You cannot 'define reality'. You act in accordance with 'reality' as you see it or believe it to be. This means that your assumptions and prejudices affect how you think and act. Your own abilities will increase as you adapt your perception of what you believe you are capable of.

Cognitive Dissonance

Ye canna haud twa thochts in yer heid aat conter each ither. Ye'll git fasht an hasht fan fit ye troo is back-speird. Fit ye think an fit wye ye see thingies canna be contrar – een or th'ither maun gee wye.

You can't hold two thoughts in your head, which contradict each other. You will be troubled and harassed when what you believe is questioned. What you think and how you see things can't be at odds – one or other must give way.

▲ A person cannot hold two contradictory attitudes of beliefs at the same time. Anxiety arises when a belief is challenged. So, if a belief is contradicted by a new perception, we must change our belief or adjust our perception.

A smert-erse is nae aawyes smert. Dinna haud back gin ye hae yer doots.

A clever clogs is not always clever. Don't hold back if you have your doubts.

▲ This does not mean that we are wrong – it may just be that we have to accept that 'experts' and 'best practice' are not necessarily logical or justified. You may be right!

Fair doos, myne there's aye a chunce aat ye'll mak a cuddy o things eence in a filie.
To be fair, remember there is always a chance that you'll make a mess of things once in a while.
▲ Equally, you must be prepared to admit that you are wrong.

Gin there's a muckle gap atween faur ye are noo an faur ye're gyaan, yer heid will aye fin a wye o gettin ye ower't.
If there is a wide gap between where you are now and where you are going, your head will always find a way of getting over the gap.
▲ If there is a big gap between current reality and the vision or goal, you will subconsciously create the energy to work out how to bridge the gap.

Div ye mind fit it wis like ti dee ae thing aat gied ye a guid conceit o yersel? Picter fit ye're needin ti dee an hae a thochtie aboot fit it felt lik ti dee the ither thing.
Do you remember what it felt like to do something which you are proud of? Picture what you are wanting to do and think about what it felt like to do the other thing.
▲ Associate the emotion associated with a past success to help condition you for a future achievement – visualise the achievement and associate it with the emotion of an earlier (unrelated) success.

Fit we see is nivver the hale picter.
What we see is never the whole picture.
▲ Our perception of reality is limited.

***There's ower muckle facks gyaan aboot fir us ti hunnle
it aa bi thinkin aboot it. We've a riddle in wir heids aat
kin tell fit maiters – nae foo muckle.***

There is always too much information in circulation for
us to handle it all by thinking about it. We have a sieve
in our heads which can identify what matters rather
than how much information there is.

▲ But there is too much information for us to handle
  it all consciously. We have a subconscious filter
  in the brain which allows through to our
  consciousness only what we have decided is
  important or a threat. It is not the quality or quantity
  of the information that is important but its
  significance.

***Aat means aat gin ye hiv decided fit maiters ti ye,
the riddle sees til't aat the facks aat maiter git
throwe.***

That means that, if you have decided what matters to
you, the sieve ensures that the information that matters
gets through.

▲ So, if you set a goal, you are deciding what is to be
  significant for you. Your 'filter' lets through
  information which will help you achieve the goal.
  Sometimes the information is already there.

***Gin ye dinna hae a gweed conceit o yersel, ye'll aye
need ti ken aat aathing will be jist dandy afore ye git
roadit.***

If you don't have confidence in yourself, you will
always need to know that everything will be perfect
before you get started.

▲ Low self esteem means you want a guarantee of
  success before setting out.

Maist o fit hauds us back we pit oan oor ain shooders.
Most of what holds us back we place on our own
shoulders.
▲ Most of our limitations are self-imposed.

*Faain ower fair learns ye a thing or twa. Gin ye dinna
fa ower files, ye're nae takkin big eneuch steps.*
Falling over fairly teaches you a thing or two. If you
don't fall over now and again, you aren't taking big
enough steps.
▲ Failure is a powerful means of learning. If you do not
  fail occasionally, your goals are too small.

Gie yersel a gweed conceit of yersel.
Tell yourself how good you are.
▲ Control your self talk so that it is positive.

*Ither fowk dinna ken us – and we dinna ken ither fowk.
Ye dinna ken fit they ken, fit they're thinkin, faur they've
bin nor faur they're gyaan nor fit maiters til them.*
Other people don't know us – and we don't know other
people. You don't know what they know, what they are
thinking, where they have been, where they are going
or what is important to them.
▲ Others do not know us – and we do not know
  others. You cannot, therefore, compare yourself to
  someone else.

*Gin ye canna git a haud o fit yer heid's sayin til ye, it's
got a haud o ye.*
If you can't get a hold of what your head is saying to
you, it's taken hold of you.
▲ If you do not control your self-talk, it will control
  you.

COMPUTERS AND TECHNOLOGY

MICROSOFT ERROR MESSAGES AND HAIKU POETRY

Japanese-style Haiku poetry has only three lines and seventeen syllables – five syllables in the first line, seven in the second, five in the third. The internet has a number of examples of suggested replacements for standard Microsoft Error messages with Haiku poetry messages.

> *Yer file wis muckle.*
> *Mebbe handy an aa, like.*
> *But it's awa noo.*
> Your file was very large.
> Maybe useful as well, you know.
> But it is away now.
> ▲ Your file was so big.
>   It might be very useful.
>   But now it is gone.

> *The page ye're aifter*
> *Is naewye ti bi seen, but*
> *There's mair gyaan aboot.*
> The page you're after
> Is nowhere to be seen, but
> There are more in circulation.
> ▲ The web site you seek
>   Cannot be located, but
>   Countless more exist.

It's aa a richt rummle.
Hae a thinkie, then rebeet.
It'll aa come richt.
It's all a real mess.
Have a think, then reboot.
It will all come right.
▲ Chaos reigns within.
  Reflect, repent and reboot.
  Order shall return.

Saftware's faan ower.
It's lowsin time fir aathin.
Ye're ower gutsy.
Software has fallen over.
It's time to stop for everything.
You are over greedy.
▲ Program aborting:
  Close all that you have worked on.
  You ask far too much.

Windaes NT's deid.
It's awa til the knackery.
Ye're oan yer ain noo.
Windows NT is dead.
It is away to the slaughterhouse.
You are on your own now.
▲ Windows NT crashed.
  I am the Blue Screen of Death.
  No one hears your screams.

Yestreen it wid ging.
The day we're richt oot o luck.
Windaes aye dis aat.
Yesterday it would go.
Today we are right out of luck.
Windows always does that.

[97]

▲ Yesterday it worked.
   Today it is not working.
   Windows is like that.

A pucklie snaa, syne
The hale screen's aa gaed awa.
It wis bonnie, myne.
A wee bit of snow, then
The whole screen all went away.
It was attractive, though.
▲ First snow, then silence.
   This thousand-dollar screen dies
   So beautifully.

It's naewye in sicht.
Yon bumf ye chappit in eence
Needs chappit eence mair.
It's nowhere in sight.
That document you keyed once.
Needs keyed in once more
▲ Having been erased,
   The document you're seeking
   Must now be retyped.

Hing on a mintie.
Aathing's gaed heelster gowdie.
It's a richt scunner.
Hang on a minute.
Everything has gone upside down.
It's a real nuisance.
▲ Serious error.
   All shortcuts have disappeared.
   Screen. Mind. Both are blank.

Neen seen fan ye seek.
Jist nithin ava ti spy.
Error 'Bumf nae wye'.
None seen when you seek.
Just nothing at all to catch sight of.
Error 'Document nowhere'.
▲ With searching comes loss
   And the presence of absence:
   Error 'File not found'.

Spikkin aboot fit?
Error: 'It's aa fair connacht'.
Ach, A'm awa hame.
Saying what?
Error: 'It's all quite worn out.'
Oh, well, I am away home.
▲ 'This is a permanent error'
   I've given up.
   Sorry it didn't work out.

Haud yer haun the noo.
There's nae pynt chaan yer heid aff.
Aathin's jist knackered.
Hold your hand just now.
There is no point chewing your head off.
Everything has had it.
▲ Stay the patient course.
   Of little worth is your ire.
   The network is down.

Aa yon sillar, an
Yer fantoosh kist o furlies
Hing's jist lik a steen.
All that money, and
Your fancy PC
Hangs just like a stone.

▲ A crash reduces
Your expensive computer
To a simple stone.

Ye're nivver sure bit
Ye'll dee, pey tax an lose bumf.
Fit een is't ivnoo?
You are never sure other than
You will die, pay tax and lose data.
Which one is it right now?
▲ Three things are certain:
Death, taxes and lost data.
Guess which has occurred.

Ye dip yer tae in.
Losh, min – but it's nae een weet.
'Error fower oh fower'.
You dip your toe in.
Goodness, man – but it's not even wet.
'Error 404'.
▲ You step in the stream,
But the water has moved on.
This page is not here.

Myne oot. Oot o myne.
Get a haud o aathin blae?
Nae chunce o aat, min.
Watch out. Forgotten.
Get a hold of all things blue.
No chance of that, man
▲ Out of memory.
We wish to hold the whole sky,
But we never will.

MICROSOFT ERROR MESSAGES

The following error messages can all be found on the Microsoft
web site (you may have encountered some yourself!). Some
make more sense than others . . .

Bumf nae wye
Document nowhere (to be found)
▲ File not found

Fa's bletherin?
Who is gossiping?
▲ The phone line is busy

A'm nae needin a news wi onybody the day – pit Metal Mickey on richt noo
I'm not wanting to pass the time of day with anyone
today – put the modem on right now
▲ A person answered instead of a modem

Hiv we nae peyed wir sub? We're cut aff
Have we not paid our subscription? We're cut off
▲ The account has expired

Gie's a haun ti get the cork out, will ye?
Give us a hand to get the cork out, will you?
▲ Could not initialise port

An ye think A'm chuffed aboot it?
And you think that *I* am pleased about it?
▲ Iexplore.exe has encountered a problem and needs
to close. We are sorry for the inconvenience

IE's intimmers is aa in a guddle
Internet Explorer's 'internals' are all in a mess
▲ Microsoft Internet Explorer. There was an internal
error

A canna see fit wye ti ging
I can't see which way to go
▲ Path not found

It's jist as weel A didnae find the path, then
It's just as well I didn't find the path, then
▲ The destination is unreachable

Damn't. Dr Stephen got ti the bottle afore us!
Damn it. My former rugby team mate got to the bottle before us!
▲ Port already open

Aat's the bluidy Spanish again – geein it laldie jist cos the Fergie's f****d!
That's the bloody Spanish again – celebrating noisily just because the Ferguson (tractor) is not working
▲ OLE Automation Error

Perkins is aff!
Scots crumbly ginger biscuits are not on the menu
▲ Your web browser options are currently set to disable cookies

Ye'll jist hae ti get oot the clubbie buik aifter aa
You will just have to get the mail order catalogue out after all
▲ Failed to install catalogue files

Bluidy richt A'm objecting!
Too right I am objecting!
▲ Runtime error, Line 0, object expected

The stook's faan ower
The haystack has fallen over
▲ Stack Overflow

Mebbe he's awa fir his fly iv noo – he'll be readin the funcy paper
Perhaps he is away for a cup of tea at the moment – he'll be reading the high quality paper
▲ The printer cannot be found

An the monitor's munkie, the printer's yirdid an the keyboard's fair clartit
And the monitor is dirty, the printer is very dirty and the keyboard is absolutely covered in muck
▲ The disk is full
(Note: *full* also means dirty or foul.)

Ess widna wash in the NHS, wid it? Is't jist th'expectit eens ye kin cope wi?
This wouldn't wash in the NHS, would it? Is it just the expected ones you can cope with?
▲ The current operation could not be completed because an unexpected error has occurred

Oh aye? An A'm Wullie Gates's grunnie . . .
Oh yes? And I'm Bill Gates's grandmother . . .
▲ Your password must be at least 18770 characters long and cannot repeat any of your previous 30689 passwords

An fit gin it's nae aa richt?
And what if it's *not* OK?
▲ The memory could not be read. Click OK to terminate the program

Aat's Foresterhill's waiting lists b*gg*r'd up again, than
That's the local NHS Trust's waiting lists messed up again, then
▲ An operation is pending

Is aa wives the same?
Are all wives the same?
▲ Argument not optional

Nae chunce
No chance
▲ Permission denied

Is 'Nae chunce' nae clear eneuch?
Is 'No chance' not clear enough?
▲ Expression too complex

The lumpie's lichtit bit there's naebody hame
The light is on but there is no one at home
▲ There was no answer

Gin life (an Windaes) wis aat easy . . .
If only life (and Windows) was that easy . . .
▲ To avoid seeing this message again, always shut
down your computer by selecting shut down from
the start menu

INFORMATION TECHNOLOGY AND
BUSINESS SYSTEM TERMINOLOGY

Kist o furlies wheechin roon an roon
Chest (box) of wheels going round and round at speed
▲ Computer

Interwheecher
(High speed) connections between computers
▲ Internet
(Both courtesy of Gordon Casely's in-depth knowledge
of modern technology.)

Gyaan fae Cockbridge ti Tomintoul in blin drift
Going over The Lecht in a blizzard
▲ Hard drive

A roch chiel fa eeses sweirie wirds
An uncouth man who swears
▲ Cursor

Noo an again
Occasionally
▲ Files

The Files loon
The young son of the Whiles family
▲ Master files

Ach, it wis in ma heid jist a mintie syne
Oh dear, it was in my head just a minute ago
▲ Memory stick

Haud baith feet on the fleer an dinna rax oot ower far aat ye cowp
Keep both feet on the floor and don't over-reach so that you fall over
▲ Work Level Instruction

Orra loons aawye
Unskilled farm workers everywhere
▲ Server Farm

A buik aat tells ye aa aboot the currots an neeps, faur they bide an fit nummer ye kin gie them a phonie at
A publication which gives you the contact details of certain vegetables
▲ Root directory

A bit like clarty dubs
Rather like sticky mud
▲ GUI (graphical user interface)

The kist o furlies aat May Dow eeses ti haud the recipes fir hir aifter-dinner sweeties aat she maks fir Stew Spence (the 'Goulash Gadgie' o European slow-cooking circles) at the Marcliffe ootbye Pitfodels
The computer May Dow uses to make the after-dinner tablet served by the owner of our local 'Small Luxury Hotel of the World'
▲ Tablet PC

Faur's yon quine fae the agency? A tellt them we aye git yokit bi 8.30
Where is the interim receptionist? I told the agency that we always start at 8.30
▲ Template

Brummle in yer haun
Bramble in your hand
▲ Hand-held Blackberry

Faur an aul wifie pits her hair
Where an elderly woman puts her hair
▲ Internet

Faur a fitba gings in Glesca
Where a football goes in Glasgow
▲ Intranet

As far awa fae 'gross' as ye kin ging
As far away from 'gross' as you can get
▲ Extranet

Lay-aff dyke
Downsize dyke
▲ Firewall

Fair skelpit
Well beaten
▲ Number of Hits

Hilly Billies' buggy
Aberdeen Mountain Rescue Team landrover
▲ Search Engine

Fit the Cod Crusaders are efter savin
What the Cod Crusaders want to preserve
▲ Network

Ma faither's claymore
My father's fighting weapon
▲ Password

Fit ye canna dee fir fun nooadays
A sport you can no longer participate in
▲ Firefox

Reid deer
Red deer
▲ Browser

The snaa's awa fae the Howe
Spring in the Howe of Alford
▲ Brownfield site

Runnin Craiginches
Running Aberdeen prison
▲ Agile business

Fit ye git fan yer knicker elastick's ower ticht
What you get when the elastic in your pants is too tight
▲ The bottom line

It's naethin ti dee wi a funcy lettuce
It has no connection with salad leaves
▲ It ain't rocket science

Dinna be sae cheeky, ye twa-faced nickum
Get your bum off the photocopier, you two-faced rascal
▲ Do not abuse the office equipment at the Christmas
   party

TEXT MESSAGING IN THE NORTH-EAST

KI – Ken is?
Have you heard what I've just heard?

YK – Ye ken
You know

Y2K – Ye baith ken
You both know

FAP – Funcy a pint?
Shall we adjourn to the Dutch Mill?

FFFFFFW? – Faur, fit, fan, fa, foo, fit wye?
Where, what, when, who, how, why?

FWWAK – Fit wye wid A ken?
How on earth would I know?

AYFG – Awa ye feel gype
Away you go, stupid idiot

GTF – G'wa ti Foggie
Take yourself off elsewhere and lose yourself – as often
suggested by Bill Mackie in a slightly more direct fashion

AJA – At's jist affa
That is just terrible

THJBONA – The hale jing bang or nithin ava
All or nothing

YHHYT – Ye'll hae hid yer tea?
You will have had your tea? (more of a statement than a
question)

SAYK – Sae aat ye ken
So that you know (same as For your information (FYI))

E-MAIL ETIQUETTE

Dinna keep yer bunnet lockit up – it's jist lik baalin at fowk.
Set CAPS LOCK off – upper case is just like shouting at people.

Dinna chap gin yer chaffed. Haud yer wheesht if ye're nae richt sure
Don't email if you are angry. You will probably say something you will regret.

Gin twa-three wirds is eneuch, twa-three wirds is eneuch. Dinna e-blether.
If you can say it in a few words, say it in a few words. Don't be electronically wordy.

Dinna hae a muckle story aboot fa ye are.
Keep signatures down to fewer than six lines.

Gin ye canna mak't clear aat ye're funnin, say it anither wye. Dinna use thae gypit 'emoticon' thingies fir ony sake – naebody kens fit they aa mean.
If you can't make it clear that you're being funny, rewrite it. Don't use those silly 'emoticons' – no one knows what they all mean (as will be demonstrated in the following chapter).

Dinna be a short-erse.
If you must use abbreviations or acronyms, be sure that your reader knows what they stand for.

Mak siccar aat fit ye're sayin is richt afore ye forrit it til onybody else.
Check with sources before distributing information.

Spam's nae fine ti eat.
Unsolicited email is an unpalatable feature of the internet.

Myne oot fir the fowk ye're emailin til. Mebbe they dinna hae a muckle wire nor a funcy kist o furlies, sae attachments tak aa day ti git there an yer HTML message cams oot as sae muckle haivers. Gin it's a muckle file, speir at em first afore ye chap oan 'Send'.
Be aware that your recipients may not have a fast connection, a compatible e-mail program or a sophisticated computer, so that attachments take a long time to download and your HTML message is unintelligible. If it is a large file, ask them first before you hit 'Send'.

Spell oot fit ye're spikkin aboot.
Use the 'Subject' field to describe the content of your message.

Dinna ignore fowk. It's nae as if ye're deif.
Don't ignore (valid) incoming messages. If the message gets through, why not show some common decency and reply?

Dinna chap onythin ye widna spik oot loud.
Don't type anything you wouldn't say in public.

Dinna be coorse.
Don't be offensive.

Files, gie yer files a gweed redd up.
Occasionally, tidy up your mail folders.

Dinna speir fir a 'reply receipt' gin ye dinna need't – and dinna say ti hash on wi't gin there's nae rush.
Don't ask for a 'reply receipt' if you don't need it – and don't say something is urgent if it isn't.

EMOTICONS

;-) *Eye aye, min!*
A typical north-east greeting

:-(*A'm nae affa chuffed*
I am not very pleased

:-> *A think A'm Airchie*
I think I am wonderful (but others call me smug!)

:-\ *A'm nae richt sure*
I am not completely certain

:-| *A'm nae aat fussed*
I am indifferent

:-& *Ma tongue's aa knottit*
I am tongue-tied

|-| *A'm asleep*
I am asleep

:-# *Ma mou's ticht shut*
My lips are sealed

*-| *Michty me – A'm fair flummoxed!*
Goodness me – I am quite at a loss

:-< *A'm near ti greetin*
I am almost in tears

:-{} *A'm a Clarty Tartie – ma mou's aa reid*
I have insufficient confidence in my natural charm and
beauty that I feel the need to apply copious amounts of
lipstick in the (mistaken) belief that it will ensure
success in the romantic arena

8-# *A'm deid!*
I am dead

:-I *A'm nae sayin nithin*
Hmmm

:-x *Gie's a kiss!*
Give us a kiss!

:-7 *A've jist makkit up some Haiku poetry (wis't ful?)*
I have just composed some (wistful) Haiku poetry (was it dirty?)

:-p *A'm stickin ma tongue oot at ye*
I am sticking my tongue out at you

:-* *Michty me bit yon vinegar in the Baxter's beetreet's affa soor*
Goodness but that vinegar in the Baxter's beetroot is very sour

;>) *A canna help haein a muckle neb – an ye thocht Concorde wis groundit*
I can't help having a large nose – and you thought that Concorde was grounded

%-) *Ma boxers is a bit oan the ticht side*
My underpants are rather tight

#-) *A've a hingower – ma heid's dirlin*
I have a hangover – my head is vibrating

[:-) *A canna hear ye – ma lugs is wired intil Fred MacAulay*
I can't hear you – my ears are connected by headphones to the *Fred MacAulay Show*

(-: *Look at it ess wye roon*
Look at it this way round

:- *Wullie*
Willie

}:-(*A've a bug run oan ma heid*
I have a central hair parting

{(:-) *A've a rug oan ma heid*
I wear a toupee

}(:-(*Ma rug's aboot ti tak aff – it's aat drauchtie*
My toupee is about to take off – it is so windy

:-} *A've a mowser lik Dowser*
I have a moustache like that of Major John Dow, retired Gordon's College PE master, CCF officer and rugby referee

@:I *Kin Tilly nae bundage ma heid better nor is?*
Can Sister Thomas not bandage my head better than this?

8-) *Fowk caa me Specky*
My sight is not what it was

:-)8 *It's nae jist Johnnie Macrae fa weirs a bow tie, ken*
It is not just the chairman of Aberdeen Solicitors Property Centre who wears a bow tie, you know

:-0 *A'm aye gabbin*
I speak a lot

:-o *A'm aye gobbin*
Expectoration is common

={:-) *I askit Jeff fir a Nummer 3 – it looks mair lik a 24/7 ti me. Is aat his noshun o Shape'n'Style?*
I asked the barber for a 'Number 3' haircut – it looks more like a 24 on top and 7 back and sides to me. Is this where he got the idea for his barber's shop name?

*<|:-) *A'm Suntie Claas (Hyow, hyow, hyow!)*
I am Father Christmas (Hoe, hoe, hoe!)

AND FINALLY . . .

After my father died, I found a copy of the following poem by Hugh Barrie in my father's own handwriting among his papers. It comes from *Poems of the Scottish Hills*, edited by Hamish Brown (AUP). This is my translation.

FAN A'M DEID
Fin A'm awa,
An the unco spirk o smeddum in ma breist
His fleed awa ti jyne the muckle fite hert o life
Aat maun fairly birstle ayont us aa,
An aathin aat ivver wis maasel
Is jist foost an caul deid stoor,
Fin eence A hid a gweed conceit o maasel, noo
Teen awa fir ivvermair.

Fir ony's sake, dinna cast me aneth the grun
Awa fae the licht an the couthieness o life:
Bit tak ma fitened banes til the heid o the glen;
Oot o the steer an stramash o the toon,
Fynd a muckle steen faur the win aye blaas,
An on't jist lay me doon,
Faur the scree skites doon ti the dreich dumpness,
An the snaamelt shines fite agin the blaik, blaik steens,
Sypin wi smirr in a caul, caul win:
An the lichtsome licht o the sin disna ging.
Faur the hicht o the ben wid ding doon the hivvins: an aa
The ongyauns o mortal chiels are fair
Oot o myn.

Jist sae aat A ken,
Fan A've weert awa as aabody maun,

The seelent sough o slantin sleet an snaa:
The stoonin o hale watter: the coorse rowt o stags:
The skelp o the snell win: an still an oan
The canny skreek o the day will kep the bluidless banes
Faur eence bade ma een: an A'll see the sindoon,
An syne A'll ken the douce cannieness o nicht
An o the stars A'll hae a sicht.

WHEN I AM DEAD
When I am away
And the strange spark of liveliness in my breast
Has fled to join the great white heart of life
That must surely scorch beyond us all
And everything that ever was myself
Is just mould and cold dead dust
When once I had a good conceit of myself, now
Taken away for evermore.

For any sake, don't bury me beneath the ground
Away from the light and the friendliness of life:
But take my whitened bones to the head of the glen
Out of the bustle and commotion of the town
Find a large stone where the wind always blows,
And on it just lay me down,
Where the small stones on the slope slip down to the dreary
dampness,
And the water from the melting snow shines white against the
black black stones,
Soaked with drizzle in a cold, cold wind;
And the friendly light of the sun doesn't go.
Where the height of the hill would bring down the heavens;
and all
The ongoings of mortal people are right
Out of mind.

Just so that I know,
When I have worn away as everyone must,
The silent sigh of slanting sleet and snow:
The sharp pain of torrential rain: the rough roar of stags:
The slap of the chilling wind: and still
The gentle break of day will touch the bloodless bones
Where once lived my eyes: and I'll see the sundown,
And then I'll know the soft gentleness of night
And of the stars I'll have a sight.

▲ When I am dead,
And this strange spark of life that in me lies
Is fled to join the great white core of life
That surely flames beyond eternities,
And all I ever thought of as myself
Is mouldering to dust and cold dead ash,
This pride of nerve and muscle – merest dross,
This joy of brain and eye and touch but trash,
Bury me not, I pray thee,
In the dark earth, where comes not any ray
Of light or warmth or ought that made life dear:
But take my whitened bones far, far away
Out of the hum and turmoil of the town,
Find me a wind-swept boulder for a bier,
And on it lay me down,
Where far beneath drops sheer the rocky ridge
Down to the gloomy valley, and the streams
Fall foaming white against black beetling rocks
Where the sun's kindly radiance seldom gleams:
Where some tall peak, defiant, steadfast, rocks
The passing gods: and all the ways of men
Forgotten.

So may I know
Even in that death that comes to everything
The swiftly silent swish of hurrying snow:
The lash of rain: the savage bellowing
Of stags: the bitter keen-knife-edge embrace
Of the rushing wind: and still the tremulous dawn
Will touch the eyeless sockets of my face:
And I shall see the sunset and anon
Shall know the velvet kindness of the night
And see the stars.